D0853006

THE POWER OF PROGRESS

THE POWER OF PROGRESS

How America's Progressives Can (Once Again)
Save Our Economy, Our Climate, and Our Country

JOHN PODESTA
WITH JOHN HALPIN

Crown Publishers

New York

Copyright © 2008 by Center for American Progress

All rights reserved.

Published in the United States by Crown Publishers, an imprint of the
Crown Publishing Group, a division of Random House, Inc., New York.

www.crownpublishing.com

CROWN and the Crown colophon are registered trademarks of Random House, Inc.

Library of Congress Cataloging-in-Publication Data

Podesta, John.

The power of progress: how America's progressives can (once again) save our economy,
our climate, and our country / John Podesta with John Halpin.

    p.   cm.

Includes bibliographical references and index.

    I. Democratic Party (U.S.)   2. Progressivism (United States politics)   3. United
States—Politics and government—1989— I. Title.

JK2316. P63 2008

324.2736—dc22

2008016543

ISBN: 978-0-307-38255-9

Printed in the United States of America

DESIGN BY LEONARD W. HENDERSON

10 9 8 7 6 5 4 3 2 1

First Edition

To Megan, Mae, and Gabe,

who are living their dreams and

working to build a more just and peaceful world

CONTENTS

THE POWER OF PROGRESS

Why I Am a Progressive

As I sat down to reflect on progressive politics in the last century and this new one, it struck me that it's not a surprise that I am a progressive—I was born to it. I grew up in Chicago, but my father wasn't an elected official or even a precinct captain. Like millions of other Americans in the twentieth century, however, we were able to crawl our way up the ladder and achieve the American Dream because progressive politicians and policies made it possible.

The progressive values that defined our national life during most of the twentieth century allowed my family—poor Italian and Greek immigrants transplanted to America—to flourish and prosper. From the time I was a kid (usually when I had gotten in trouble), my mother sat me down at the kitchen table—after she came home from working the night shift—and reminded me that because I had so much I owed something back. I thought at the time that we didn't have much of anything. But, she had lived through the Depression and she was right. We did have something. Progressive values had allowed families who had arrived in America with little more than the clothes they wore to get jobs and earn a piece of the American Dream—just as these policies and the opportunity they gave families like ours helped America become the greatest nation on earth.

Owing something back means making sure that this is a country where *every* generation of Americans has the opportunities we did—both established families and newcomers to these shores.

My family's story is hardly unique, but it embodies what made America a beacon of hope and gives us the potential to be not only a military power but a moral leader. And it's worth remembering, at a time when the immigration debate has become poisoned by anger, that the immigrants arriving today are a lot like my own forebears were: poor, uneducated, unable to speak English—and capable of making a great nation even greater. I'm in politics today because I think it's important that all American families continue to have the opportunity to live stories like my family's—and because I believe that the conservatives running this country today not only don't seem to care much if those families do succeed, they don't seem to have any understanding at all of what working people's lives are really like.

This nation has been led off course by leaders who have proven unable to understand or implement the most basic conception of this American experience. Conservatism cannot lead the way because it has already failed. And the challenges that our nation faces are simply too dramatic to allow for failure again.

Our nation's best way forward—in fact, our only way forward—is to recapture and reassert progressive values.

I didn't learn progressivism from books, although I've enjoyed many great historical accounts over the years. My commitment to renewing America's progressive movement comes from my background—what I learned from my family, my schools, my church, and my career.

Maybe that's why my political principles are pretty simple. Accept change and make it work for the common good. Make sure people have a chance to contribute and be rewarded for their work—give them a ladder up and they'll prosper. Teach people tolerance and compassion, and they will give back more than they receive. That's what progress means, and that's why America has always been at its greatest when our government has run on progressive ideas.

Henry Luce called the last century the "American Century." In my mind, it was the century when we finally recognized that our Constitution applied to everybody, even if they were black or poor or female; when we decided that working stiffs deserved a decent piece of the pie; working with our allies we saved the world for democracy and protected people in places we scarcely knew. And in putting progressive ideals into action on a global scale, we transformed America from an emerging power to the sole superpower and we made our people as prosperous and secure as they have ever been.

We made the twentieth century ours.

The challenges we face in this new century are as complex and profound as those we faced in the last. The global economy today burdens the poor and rewards the rich. Terrorists disrespect conventional definitions of military power and kill innocents without conscience or fear. A deteriorating climate will profoundly change the way our children live. If the twenty-first century is to be the next American Century, we will have to attack these challenges with tools rooted in the values that allowed us to triumph in the century before—values I learned almost literally at my grandmother's knees.

My grandfather Anthony was a dockworker from the hills outside of Genoa, the same city where Christopher Columbus was born. His trip to the New World didn't attract as much attention as Columbus's, but at least he actually got to where he was supposed to go: Chicago.

He lived in a walk-up tenement in downtown Chicago and worked unloading fruit and freight from railroad cars at the South Water Street market, a few blocks from the scene of the famous Haymarket riot. It wasn't a great job. Chicago's first efforts at labor organizing tended to end with riots, bombs, and massacres. Wages were nothing to write home about, even if you knew how to write.

Grandpa didn't bring much to the new world except a work ethic. It was in Chicago that he met my grandmother Francesca, who came to the States without family or a penny in her pocket. Francesca worked hard to raise six children, teaching her daughters favorite Genovese dishes such as pesto, cima, and ravioli. I still use the mortar my grandmother used to pound basil she grew on her fire escape.

Their oldest son—my father—was tall, strong, smart, and dapper. He had all of the ingredients of modern-day success, but after only a single year in high school he had to drop out to help support his family.

Dad worked in Chicago factories his entire life. It was still hard manual labor, but it was an improvement over the lives of his parents. Factories boomed, and after the Great Depression and the war, union power increased dramatically: wages rose, and people had health care and paid vacations for the first time.

My mother's parents came from the Peleponnesus, in Greece, at the turn of the century. My grandfather Louis did what so many Greek immigrants did in the United States and around the world: he went into the food business. He owned a lunch counter in downtown Chicago that could have been the original inspiration for John Belushi's skit on *Saturday Night Live*. He met my grandmother Mae in Chicago. She had left her parents, her siblings, and her village at age thirteen to travel alone to the United States to be a housekeeper. My grandparents had three great children—my mother the eldest—but their marriage was rocky and they divorced.

My mother worked in my grandfather's restaurant, and that's where she met my father. After a romance that must have been a 1930s version of *My Big Fat Greek Wedding*, they married and started a family.

Life got better: Dad and Mom were able to afford to move our family to Mayfair Park, a Northwest Side neighborhood where a factory worker could buy an apartment in what Chicagoans called a two-flat, a duplex with one apartment stacked on the other. My aunt and uncle, cousins, and grandmother lived upstairs. It had a real yard, and it was close to a public park and decent schools. My parents were doing okay.

Life in Chicago still had its rough side; like all parents, mine wanted better for my brother and me. They made us work and study hard, and when the time came, I was accepted to Lane Technical High School, a public school originally founded in 1908 to teach boys to become masons and carpenters and to work in print shops and steel mills. By the time I got there, the curriculum had changed. While I may have been one of the last students in America to take foundry for credit, in a post-Sputnik world we needed scientists and engineers as well as ironworkers and machinists. Lane Tech was where I learned my love of science. I used to say at the White House that I was the first chief of staff who knew how to surf the web, and the last who knew how to use a slide rule. Just after I graduated, admissions at Lane changed, too. They finally let girls in, to the relief of the five thousand adolescent boys who attended the school.

Because of my grades at Lane Tech, the night work I did, and access to a state scholarship and federal aid, I was able to go to Knox College and Georgetown Law School debt-free. Compare that to kids today struggling to complete community college without borrowing a small fortune.

My old neighborhood was full of respectable blue-collar families, mostly Polish, Irish, and Italian, whose lives centered on work, church, and home. But there were some people there who had brothers or children or cousins who hadn't made it out of the tenements yet, or who had fallen back, or crossed to the wrong side of the tracks and landed in jail or on the street.

That's maybe why our faith inspired us with a forgiving and compassionate Christ, the Savior who scorned earthly wealth and taught us to earn salvation when he said: "Come, blessed of my Father, into the Kingdom prepared for you from the founding of the world. For I was hungry and you fed me; I was thirsty and you gave me water; I was a stranger and you invited me into your homes; naked and you clothed me; sick and you visited me. . . . I was in prison and you came to me. As long as you did it for one of these, the least of my brethren, you did it for me."

My life was hardly unique. But what I learned growing up ethnic on the Northwest Side of Chicago became the key to being able to complete the classic multigenerational journey that went from unloading bananas from railroad cars to framing a law degree. My parents and grandparents taught me patriotism and to appreciate the unique opportunity America offered. I learned that government could make lives better for working people like my family: the New Deal meant union wages and booming factories; public schools gave me the chance to succeed, economically and intellectually. The church taught me compassion. And my dad, who never made more than $5 an hour in his life but who quite literally would give you the shirt off his back, demanded that instead of judging others, we should help feed and heal those whose needs were greater than our own.

The way they played politics in Chicago's Thirty-ninth Ward is still with me, too. They used to call Chicago "the city that works" because, for all the problems it shared with other large cities, the garbage got collected and the potholes got filled. Chicago once threw out its chief executive and elected Jane Byrne—its first woman mayor, incidentally—because her incumbent opponent didn't get the snow plowed one particularly tough winter. I like that. All the highfalutin language politicians pull out for holiday speeches, and all the dense prose of economists and academics isn't worth a damn if the garbage isn't getting picked up and the snow isn't getting plowed.

You'd think that would be obvious, but it isn't. Look at the last eight years: everything the Bush administration touches turns to dust because they're so ensnared by conservative dogma and the easy profits of crony capitalism that they can't make policy or run a government with the basic competence of a Chicago alderman. After eight years in office, more people are uninsured, more middle-class families are struggling, the housing market and banking industry are in collapse, the dollar is crashing, and a lot more people are dead in Iraq, but they refuse to change course, and their new standard bearer, John McCain, exhorts us to march on.

Another thing about Chicago politics is that people don't mind getting their hands dirty to get things done. By dirty, I don't mean dipping into the till. I hate graft, whether it's aldermen accepting briefcases full of cash or Jack Abramoff flying members of Congress to Scotland for golf. Graft makes government worse. Period. We learned about that in Chicago, too. What I mean is I don't mind twisting a few arms, or making peace with someone I don't really like, or even cutting a deal every now and then if it means getting something important done.

I think the reason I got along with Bill Clinton was that he had the same combination of progressive background and practical attitude. The president was one of the most educated and erudite people I've ever met. His idea of a good time was to spend his New Year's Eve at something called the "Renaissance Weekend" discussing the nuances of inter-American technology trade with a couple of economics professors and maybe the Ecuadorian minister of finance or the Peruvian ambassador.

When it came to government economic policy, what mattered to Bill Clinton wasn't just figures on spreadsheets or lines on a chart.

It was the people at the kitchen table late at night, looking over the bills and trying to figure out how to feed the kids and save for school or maybe buy a home of their own . . . on incomes that just didn't do the job. It was the people he grew up with as the child of a single mom in a working-class neighborhood in a small southern town— people not so different from the ones I grew up with in Chicago. Would welfare reform or a balanced budget make *their* lives better or worse? Would it give *them* more opportunity or less? Would it give hardworking average Americans a better shot at realizing the American Dream, or would it push that dream farther away? These are the questions Bill Clinton asked. And I think that's why the only time in the last thirty-five years that wages for middle-class and poor Americans rose consistently was when Bill Clinton was president—and that makes me proud of my time in the Clinton administration.

I knew where President Clinton was coming from. He understood that whatever changes sweep across the American landscape or economy, it's a good bet that the handful of people on top are going to come out okay. Factories like the ones my father worked in have been disappearing from these shores for a generation. But I'll bet most of the people who owned and ran them are still rich. And that their kids went to a good college and got their MBAs and law degrees and they're doing okay, too.

I've got no problem with that; success is good. My older brother, Tony, who went to law school like I did, stayed active in progressive politics and has done well enough that he now owns individual pieces of contemporary art that are worth more than our father earned in a decade—and several that my mother was embarrassed to be in the same room with. But that's the American Dream, isn't it? Penniless immigrant arrives in Chicago; two generations later and one grandson's meeting the president in the Oval Office and another's got a Louise Bourgeois sculpture arching over the stairway.

The reason why I founded the Center for American Progress is that we need this country to work like that for every family and we need this country to be united and strong.

Today, many who've climbed to the top of the economic ladder are trying to pull it up behind them. Business owners and managers want an ever bigger portion of the pie, leaving workers with a smaller and smaller slice. Many companies don't care if the environment is degraded as long as they hit their earning targets.

Conservative politicians are using fear and hate to divide Americans and to fan the flames of war as they push away allied governments, alienate billions of people around the world, and allow contractors to stuff their pockets. Union-busting. Gay-bashing. Race-baiting. Corner-cutting.

And after all their pious talk about religion and the soul, they never seem to get around to doing anything for the people who need help the most. They're so obsessed with Milton Friedman of Chicago that they forget the words of Jesus of Nazareth: "Blessed are the poor in spirit . . . Blessed are the meek . . . Blessed are those who hunger and thirst for justice . . . Blessed are the merciful . . . Blessed are the peace-makers."

America is experiencing a new Gilded Age, with a growing gap between the wealthy and the middle class. That gap isn't just about money. It's about dreams. It's about living in an America that truly is prosperous, safe, and free for *everyone*; where even the poorest among us see their families rise into the middle class and beyond.

When I was growing up, the idea that the rich would be getting richer while the poor were getting poorer would have been considered a moral failure, not a miracle of the marketplace. The challenge to right things will demand all the brilliance and dedication, all the new ideas and hard work, that progressive politicians can muster.

We need to build a progressive economy in which Americans at every income level share in the astonishing riches our country creates. We need a progressive environmental strategy that recognizes the environmental crisis at hand and acts to stop global warming and end America's oil addiction. And we need a national security plan that brings all nations together to fight enemies that can't be subdued by conventional weapons, and wins the hearts and minds of good people of every faith, in every nation. And we have to do it now if we don't want to find ourselves a friendless nation menaced on all sides by enemies and by terrorists—a feudal economy addicted to oil, watching helplessly as deserts expand and sea levels rise.

Globalization already threatens the livelihoods and dreams of the middle-class families who work more, earn less, and find that the costs of housing, health care, and school are spiraling out of reach.

At the same time, our addiction to fossil fuels continues to warm the atmosphere, to change the weather, to assault our forests and our crops.

We also need to reestablish our moral authority in the world. A horrifically mismanaged "war on terror" has sucked away resources, largely turned the world's 1.5 billion Muslims against America, and inspired murderous and bitter people around the world to join forces to kill innocents. At the same time, allies whose aid and support we will need to bring peace and stability to the Middle East and to contain global terror around the world have turned away from us. Six years after we rushed into an unnecessary war, we are more isolated and more vulnerable than before.

I have confidence that we can overcome these challenges. The people I grew up with, whose moms and dads overcame war and depression, raised kids as tough and smart as they were. The values they taught us—fairness, compassion, hard work, and pride in our people and our nation—are intact; they form the nucleus of a progressive movement that for a time lost its way, but hasn't lost its importance, and now is coming back. I know that young people today embrace these values; they are ready to mobilize and to help save this nation, once they hear a clarion call.

We just need ideas and activism. We need to demand leadership from political candidates and reward those with the courage to use progressive values to embrace change and make it work for us.

And that's what this book is about: providing ideas and practical leadership on the issues that most affect our lives; mobilizing the core beliefs that make us progressives and make America great; and applying them, fearlessly and directly, to the problems of the global economy, global warming, and global terror.

This is an election year, and the stakes are higher than they've been for sixty years. We need from our elected leaders what my parents and grandparents needed from theirs: an ability to accept change and to master it; a passion for reform and a commitment to openness; a determination to see that every American has an opportunity to contribute and to be rewarded; tolerance and compassion; a willingness to appeal to the national interest and the common good.

This book lays out the core beliefs of the progressive movement, tracing their historic origins as a response to the abuses and disparities of the first Gilded Age and through the great achievements of the Roosevelt and Kennedy/Johnson eras. It examines how these values played out in the Clinton years and were rejected by George W. Bush. It applies these values and searches for progressive solutions to the epochal challenges our generation faces today. It's a policy book that builds on the progressive philosophy. It's a practical guide with think-tank origins.

Perhaps most of all, it's my way of thanking my parents, and their parents, and the teachers, the priests, nuns, activists, and politicians who taught me to believe in our capacity to change and heal the world.

Because in this changing world, the solid values and progressive ideals they taught and embraced—that meant opportunity for my family and greatness for our nation—are more important than ever.

As I finished writing this manuscript, Illinois senator Barack Obama secured the Democratic Party's nomination for president, a tremendous victory for America...and, not incidentally, for my hometown. This has the potential to be a transformational moment in American history, and a transitional event in the way the rest of the world sees our country, as others have amply noted. But, for these transformations to take place, we must use the energy and excitement that this campaign and his candidacy have generated to bring needed change in our nation's direction and our government's priorities. The choice in November could hardly be clearer: between the weight of a conservative movement that has dragged this nation down, and the power of progress to restore our nation's strength and its position of moral and economic leadership. You and I will both help America make that choice; I hope this book, with its history and ideas, will help to make that choice an easy one.

PART ONE

Lessons from
Our Progressive Past

Lightning Round
(20 Seconds to Answer)
What Does It Mean
to Be a Progressive?

I do not intend to write another historical account of the Populist, Progressive, New Deal, and Great Society eras. I am neither a historian nor a social theorist, and many others before me have produced important and compelling accounts of these times. But I am a student of politics and intensely curious about how our progressive past—the men, women, leaders, ideas, and movements of previous years—shapes our understanding of progressivism today.

Whenever I'm invited to speak with activists and groups across the country, someone invariably asks, "What is progressivism?" Is it an ideology? Is it a political theory? Is it a disposition? Or is it just a political label with no real meaning? A second related question usually follows: "Isn't a progressive the same thing as a liberal?"

My answer to the first question is straightforward (and serves as the mission of the institution I founded): "Progressives believe that America should be a country of boundless opportunity, where all people can better themselves through education, hard work, fair pay, and the freedom to pursue their dreams. We believe that this will be achieved only with an open and effective government that champions the common good over narrow self-interest while securing the rights and safety of its people."

My usual response to the second question is, "Call me whatever you want." A less flippant and more historically accurate response is that liberalism and progressivism are distinct but complementary sets of ideas. They share many values and policy prescriptions but they are not exactly the same in substance, emphasis, or origin.

Liberalism throughout history has primarily focused on preserving human liberty and autonomy and protecting individual rights against encroachment by the state or society. It is a well-formulated political theory dating to the Enlightenment that has been refined over centuries in academic and government settings. As a set of ethical standards and beliefs, liberalism is frequently associated with traits such as tolerance, diversity, open-mindedness, rationality, and self-reliance. In its modern, post–New Deal form, liberalism has been chiefly concerned with achieving individual freedom in its fullest sense—freedom from undue governmental intrusion, and freedom to lead an economically secure and meaningful life.

Progressivism, on the other hand, is less theoretically developed and more hands-on in its approach. As a body of thought, progressivism is tied directly to the search for social and economic justice at the turn of the twentieth century. Unlike liberalism, there are no master texts of progressivism even though there are known progressive thinkers such as Herbert Croly and Jane Addams.[1] Political progressivism was primarily focused on breaking the control of privileged economic interests in government and restoring America to its democratic roots, where free people can live their lives and make a decent living from their labor. Progressivism as an ideological label later came into use as an umbrella concept—embraced across party and class lines—to capture a range of reform efforts from women's suffrage and the direct election of senators to public interest regulations, conservation, and social security measures.

The non-theoretical nature of progressivism derives in part

from the pragmatic origin of many of its ideas and policies. In the late nineteenth century and first part of the twentieth century, the American economy was in constant turmoil. Economic depressions were frequent, agricultural work was unstable, and workers faced tremendous hurdles in getting decent pay and working conditions. Widespread poverty and political corruption were real threats to the American way of life. Something had to be done to fix these problems, and the theoretical defense for government action on behalf of people could come later. My parents weren't interested in economic theory—they were interested in putting food on the table during the Great Depression, and getting their kids into a decent public school.

Progressivism was thus rooted in a fierce moral vision of what is right and wrong in society. For progressives, ensuring that people have enough to eat and that kids get a decent chance in life is right. Exploiting workers and using child labor is wrong. Supporting people who work hard and do their part is right. Leaving people vulnerable to the whims of economic forces beyond their control is wrong. "Irish need not apply" signs are wrong. Full equality and opportunity for all is right.

For some progressives, this moral vision is highly theoretically or theologically based, as was the case with turn-of-the-century social scientists such as Richard Ely and Charles Beard or with Social Gospel Protestants such as Walter Rauschenbusch and social justice Catholics such as Monsignor John Ryan and Mother Cabrini, who played an important role for the Italian immigrants in Chicago of my grandparents' generation. But unlike socialists or laissez-faire conservatives (the two ideological extremes at the time), progressives tended to avoid dogmatism in determining how best to legislate and support their moral vision. The experimentation of the New Deal best personifies the progressive commitment to pragmatism grounded in core beliefs about equal opportunity in society.

Turn-of-the-century reformers, like those of today, were motivated by concrete problems—declining crop prices, home foreclosures, paltry wages, long work hours, or Pinkertons beating down union drives. Progressives wanted democracy restored and economic security extended to the masses. They wanted government to be open, transparent, committed to public needs, and focused on helping people make the most of their lives. Progressives wanted reforms that worked to correct these problems and protected ordinary people. They didn't particularly care how or in what form the nation got there. Some progressives wanted to return to a Jeffersonian, republican ideal of small producers and individual freedom that attacked both big government and big corporations. Others wanted a stronger national government to regulate and challenge the prevailing economic powers at the time for the benefit of workers and the nation as a whole.[2]

Some people who identify with the values I've just described prefer to call themselves liberals. And it's true that after the New Deal, the liberal and progressive projects were closely aligned and the use of the two terms came to embody similar themes and policy prescriptions. Progressivism and liberalism are clearly part of a common project, standing in opposition to conservatism, and designed to improve the lives of everyday Americans by increasing both economic security and economic opportunity.

But given my background and my pragmatic beliefs, I prefer to identify with the distinctly progressive spirit that marked the reform period of around 1890–1920. This is the period of my grandparents' arrival in Chicago and the time when the most significant reforms and ideas about activist government were put into practice. The original Progressive era serves as a useful and inspiring historical moment in helping to understand the challenges we face today.

When comparing this Progressive era to the classical and modern forms of liberalism, there are four primary distinctions that are informative:

- *Faith.* Liberalism is strongly grounded in religious pluralism and the reduction of religious conflict in society. This stems directly from the religious wars of Europe that the Founding Fathers hoped to avoid in America. The liberal perspective leads directly to our First Amendment protections of religious freedom and the separation of church and state as a means to protect both religion and the government from unwarranted intrusion. In contrast, progressivism and many progressive leaders at the turn of the century were far more grounded in specific religious ethics and the social application of religious teachings to politics and society. Progressive Christianity and progressive Judaism have informed reform movements from abolition to women's suffrage to civil rights.
- *The role of government.* Liberalism, post–New Deal, is intimately associated with the rise and defense of federal government action. Progressivism, however, began at the municipal level (for example, the anti-corruption and utility reform efforts of the great cities) before moving on to larger efforts in statehouses and governors' offices. Progressives later took their reform ideas to the federal level as the need for collective efforts on conservation, social protections, and corporate regulations grew beyond their reach. This movement from the local to the federal level is best exemplified in the legislative achievements of Theodore Roosevelt and Robert La Follette. Liberalism's later focus

on federal government action, most commonly associated with FDR and the New Deal, was therefore the culmination of decades of progressive activism and legislative efforts across all levels of society and government. It is equally important to note that progressivism has a rich nongovernmental tradition based in the settlement movement and other community-based efforts to improve living conditions for the poor and less educated members of society.

- *Partisanship*. Liberalism, in its post–New Deal form, is also closely tied to the Democratic Party and, in particular, the presidencies of FDR, Truman, Kennedy, and Johnson. Progressivism, in contrast, emerged as a non-partisan reform effort that sought to clean up corruption and stop the servicing of special interests in both political parties. Progressivism's main goal was to keep politicians on both sides of the aisle honest and committed to principled actions on behalf of regular Americans. The embrace of "progressive" as a label was perhaps most prevalent among Republican Party reformers such as Teddy Roosevelt, Robert La Follette, and Albert Cummins as they tried to break up the corporate machines that dominated the Republican Party. Dissatisfied with the lack of change in the party, both TR and La Follette later ran as strong third-party candidates for president under the banner of the Progressive Party.

- *Community versus individualism*. In terms of theoretical distinctions, liberalism in all its forms is very much focused on individualism and the rights and opportunities of individuals in society. For conservative liberals today (libertarians), this means minimal government intervention in the economy and in private lives. For left-leaning liberals, this means personal freedom but also the "freedom from want," eloquently put forth by Franklin Roosevelt. Progressivism, on the other hand, is much more focused on correcting the excesses of individualism in the economy and government. In its "new nationalist" form, associated most with Herbert Croly and Teddy Roosevelt, progressive theory places much more emphasis on the importance of common purpose, national spirit, and collective needs in society and government. Progressive ethics also offers a more direct challenge to self-interest and materialism as motivators for political action than liberalism. Liberalism has focused more on diffusing the negative consequences of self-interested behavior rather than attempting to eradicate or transform it within society.

As modern progressives, most of us believe in some blending of the distinctions outlined above. We cherish both the liberal insistence on religious freedom and pluralism and the progressive moral vision that sustains political activism through more communitarian ethics and concern for others.

Over the years, I have grown into my faith with greater comfort and intensity, in a way that surprises some of my secular friends. Perhaps that is because I found a bridge between my progressive politics and my religious life at Holy Trinity parish in Georgetown, a church run by the Jesuit fathers, an order whose motto is "Men for others," that is, an order which seeks to serve the common good.

Similarly, progressives believe that the federal government must play an important role in correcting economic imbalances and in protecting individual rights, but we also believe in the importance of local actions and the primacy of communities and families in solving problems. We believe in individual rights and freedoms and in individual moral agency but also recognize the importance of a more humanitarian ethics (the Jesuit influence again) that stresses common purposes and collective responses to global problems such as poverty, climate change, and terrorism.

To better understand progressive history and thought, we must understand what drove reformers over a century ago to first challenge the political and economic order of their times. As progressive historian Eric Goldman explains, America at the turn of the twentieth century was a land of great potential and great hardship. Within a short period of time, many of the inventions that improved and enhanced everyday life for Americans were created and put into growing use—home electricity and plumbing, automobiles, telephones, and later radio. Farm prices began to increase after suffering for decades, and public education and college opportunities spread to more Americans.[3]

Despite this rising aggregate affluence, many Americans lacked basic economic security, steady employment, and humane working conditions. Corporate trusts in railroads and steel rapidly combined during this period to threaten traditional American agriculture and push more people into dangerous and poorly paid factory work. Wages for laborers did not markedly improve even as huge fortunes were amassed by J. P. Morgan and John D. Rockefeller.

The prevailing political attitude at the time was "survival of the fittest," not cooperation and government support for the working class. William Graham Sumner, a prominent social theorist and defender of laissez-faire doctrine (the Charles Murray of his time), summarized the dominant conservative beliefs of this period concisely and rather starkly:

The history of the human race is one long story of attempts by certain persons and classes to obtain control of the power of the State, so as to win earthly gratifications at the expense of others. People constantly assume that there is something metaphysical and sentimental about government. At bottom there are two chief things with which government has to deal. They are—the property of men and the honor of women.[4]

Without the progressive movement at the turn of the century, America would have been stuck in this retrograde mentality and would have remained a land of opportunity for the few and suffering for the many. The progressive transformation away from the dog-eat-dog world of the late nineteenth century defined an entirely new way of thinking about politics and government. Modern liberalism, and America as we know it today, would not exist without this progressive change.

Rather than explain progressive history in chronological order or cover every player in progressive politics (of whom there are many worth considering), I want to offer four important lessons I've taken from my reading of the progressive past. These lessons serve as core values of progressivism—unifying beliefs that have endured from the early reform days to today. Like my own version of progressivism, most of these lessons come from the practical experiences and ideas of citizens, thinkers, activists, and politicians trying to make sense of a rapidly changing world.

CHAPTER 1

LESSON ONE

Progressives Stand with People, Not Privilege

I n the fall of 1877, a self-educated former printing clerk and news-paperman, Henry George, set out to solve a profound social question afflicting late-nineteenth-century America: Why, in a time of rising material progress and wealth, was there so much "want and suffering and anxiety among the working classes"? Why is it that "where population is densest, wealth greatest, and the machinery of production and exchange most highly developed," we find "the deepest poverty, the sharpest struggle for existence, and the most enforced idleness"?[1]

The answers to these questions eventually were laid out in George's masterwork, *Progress and Poverty*, published in 1879. Although few today have heard of George and his book (including myself until I started digging into this history), in the tumultuous years around the turn of the century *Progress and Poverty* was an immensely influential work that inspired a whole generation of reform efforts in America and Europe.[2] John Kenneth Galbraith ranked George, along with Thorstein Veblen, as one of only two American political economists from the period with enduring influence. Galbraith believed that George's lasting contribution to American thought was his conclusion that "great inequality and great poverty were inevitable in the absence of great reform."[3]

For George, private land ownership was the root cause of what ailed nineteenth-century America. Like many at the time, George believed land, the earth, was a God-given resource designed to benefit all mankind—a position similar to the one many climate change activists hold today. He respected the right of owners to gain from labor and investment on their land, whether through farming or building a house or creating a factory. But he saw few benefits for society when land speculators and rail monopolies made off with undue profits supported by government franchises and handouts. In addition, as more and more of workers' wages and income went into the pockets of these speculators, marginal farmers and laborers continued to fall further behind. George saw rising inequality, destitution, and despair for the masses as the end result of speculative and often corrupt land ownership.

To end these injustices, George proposed something called the single tax—basically a uniform tax on the increased value of unimproved land that would replace all other forms of taxation. George believed the single tax was ultimately the fairest and most efficient way to fight inequality while funding necessary government works and growing the economy. As historian Robert Wiebe describes, the impetus for the single tax is perhaps clearer using my hometown as a reference: "The man who held property next to Fort Dearborn sat in a chair while society created Chicago around his plot and transformed him into a millionaire. If society claimed its own by returning the unearned value on land to all the people, injustice would disappear."[4]

Okay, you might be asking yourself, why should a modern American care about this odd theory of an underemployed printer and journalist in the late nineteenth century? Although the single tax had a limited shelf life as the solution to the problems of modern capitalism, George's approach and thinking encapsulates two important attributes of progressive politics: (1) a deep moral concern for the plight of the poor and working class, built on personal experience and Christian faith, and (2) an economic concern for how to save capitalism from its worst excesses and prevent the extremes of either socialism on the left or "survival-of-the-fittest" extremism on the right.

These attributes, if not the specific ideas, helped define an entire generation of progressive activism over the next forty years—from the rise of labor and the populists to middle-class reformers and New Dealers. Understanding this story is critical to understanding the overall progressive vision for America.

George devised his land thesis during the depression of 1873–79, the first depression associated with America's transformation from a primarily agricultural economy to an industrial one. The severity and rapidity of the economic downturn shook many Americans out of the notion that America was a perpetual land of plenty. As Eric Goldman describes:

> The years of economic distress from 1873 to 1879 threw a garish light on the whole structure of opportunity.... Millions of industrial workers, confident of a golden future a short while ago, were unemployed or desperately worried about holding their jobs. Many a small investor, once so sure of a brownstone and a carriage, found his life's savings wiped out overnight. Farmers' gilt-edged mortgage certificates turned from bright symbols of hope to nagging reminders of overconfidence. If the hard times boomed migration westward, the new pioneers passed covered wagons dragging east like whipped animals, their covers chalked with "Going back to wife's folks" or "In God we trusted, in Kansas we busted."[5]

Industrial workers were particularly harmed by these economic conditions, and, fueled by the theories of Henry George and others like him, the labor movement grew substantially during the late nineteenth century. Labor membership skyrocketed in 1885, when the half million members of the Knights of Labor successfully forced Jay Gould's rail empire to negotiate with strikers. Support for unions—and pushback against them—continued to grow after a number of violent and repressive actions by business and government against organizers.

My hometown, Chicago, a hotbed of labor activism, was the location of one particularly contentious clash: the Haymarket Square riot of 1886. Workers on strike for an eight-hour day gathered in Haymarket Square to protest police abuse. Although no one really knows what happened, someone threw a bomb at policemen trying to break up the gathering. The police opened fire on the crowd, and several people were killed and hundreds injured. After the incident, the Chicago police instigated a brutal crackdown—eight anarchists were rounded up and several eventually executed after a highly controversial trial. The violence and mistrust surrounding Haymarket heightened reactions across the country to perceived radicalism and worker unrest. As Robert Wiebe argues, there was soon a demand for more action; state militias and the U.S. Army were strengthened to respond, and quasi-vigilante "law-and-order leagues" sprang up to fight the "radicals."[6] Both established elites and middle-class citizens were concerned about the threat of foreign-born populations and the anarchist "propaganda of the deed"—bombings, killings, and other terrorist acts. Given the fear of rising violence in American communities, the reaction to these events invariably translated into the government siding with business and the wealthy against the labor movement and strikers, regardless of the circumstances.

In the Pullman strike (just south of Chicago) in 1894, workers confronted the prevailing laissez-faire spirit and the confluence of government and corporate interests. The Pullman sleeping car company employed thousands of people, many living in virtual bondage at their plant in Illinois because of strict company control of housing, wages, and basic necessities. When an economic depression in 1893 forced the company to cut wages but not costs for workers, the American Railway Union, run by Eugene Debs, went on strike and refused to operate any trains with Pullman cars. In one of the most spectacular showings of labor strength in U.S. history, nearly 100,000 rail employees stopped working—no American Railway trains were able to run from the Midwest to the West Coast.

As James Chace recounts in his overview of the strike, the company and the government were not going to let this perfidy stand. Citing vague authority over the mailing system, Democratic president Grover Cleveland authorized an injunction against the strikers and dispatched federal troops to Chicago. Although the strike had been peaceful to this point, the arrival of federal troops spurred an outbreak of violence, much of it designed to discredit the union. Despite speaking out against the violence and urging its end, Debs and other union leaders were arrested and charged with conspiracy for violating Cleveland's injunction.[7]

Cleveland's actions during the strike exemplified the typical attitude of the 1890s, when the federal government frequently sided with companies against employees fighting for decent pay and working conditions. But like Newtonian physics applied to politics, the actions of the nation's political and business elites eventually led to an equal and opposite reaction from American workers and farmers. The result was the Populist and Progressive eras. Lasting from approximately 1890 to 1920, these movements redefined American politics and profoundly altered our thinking about how our government and economy should function and for whom it should work.

Although the Populist era is often derided as an intemperate and ill-mannered agrarian revolt, it was the genesis of many of the ideas that were later enacted by twentieth-century progressive reformers and New Dealers. Offering a national platform for various reform groups and Farmers' Alliances gaining strength at the time, the People's Party (also known as the Populist Party) was launched officially on July 4, 1892, in Omaha. The Populists developed an ambitious—and at the time quite radical—reform agenda seeking to restore American democracy to its republican roots and to create a fair economy for farmers and laborers. With morally righteous language from Minnesota reformer Ignatius Donnelly, the preamble to the Omaha platform served up an unrelenting vision of a corrupted society in need of significant reordering:

> The conditions which surround us best justify our cooperation; we meet in the midst of a nation brought to the verge of moral, political, and material ruin. Corruption dominates the ballot-box, the Legislatures, the Congress, and touches even the ermine of the bench. The people are demoralized; most of the States have been compelled to isolate the voters at the polling places to prevent universal intimidation and bribery. The newspapers are largely subsidized or muzzled, public opinion silenced, business prostrated, homes covered with mortgages, labor impoverished, and the land concentrating in the hands of capitalists. The urban workmen are denied the right to organize for self-protection, imported pauperized labor beats down their wages, a hireling standing army, unrecognized by our laws, is established to shoot them down, and they are rapidly de-

generating into European conditions. The fruits of the toil
of millions are boldly stolen to build up colossal fortunes
for a few, unprecedented in the history of mankind; and the
possessors of those, in turn, despise the republic and endanger liberty. From the same prolific womb of governmental injustice we breed the two great classes—tramps
and millionaires.[8]

Donnelly's words still resonate today. At the time, it was a necessary call to arms against an economy and government overrun by selfishness, greed, and graft. The Populists saw society divided along stark
moral lines. As historian Richard Hofstadter explains, on the bad side
for populists were "the allied hosts of monopolies, the money power,
great trusts and railroad corporations," and on the good side were "the
farmers, laborers, merchants, and all other people who produce
wealth and bear the burdens of taxation . . . Between these two there
is no middle ground."[9]

To challenge the economic elites head-on, the Omaha platform
spelled out a principle of governance that departed dramatically
from the brand of liberalism and Republican rule that had defined
America since the end of the Civil War: "We believe that the
power of government—in other words, of the people—should be
expanded . . . as rapidly and as far as the good sense of an intelligent
people and the teachings of experience shall justify, to the end that
oppression, injustice, and poverty shall eventually cease in the land."

It's difficult to overstate the importance of this shift of thinking. To move from the small-government, hands-off spirit of America's roots—the quintessential Jeffersonian stance that had defended
America's rural heritage and republican virtues for a century—to a
position of maximum expansion of government (within the boundaries of common sense) to intervene on behalf of society's marginal

members was a minor revolution in political thought. As Jack Beatty summarizes in his recent book on the era,

> In the Gilded Age it was easier to credit the virgin birth than that government could serve the general welfare. Republican government serviced business. The Democrats wanted a weak federal government so that the southern oligarchy could maintain the institutions—lynching, convict labor, fraudulent elections, disenfranchisement, racial apartheid— that alone gave it popular legitimacy. The Populist credo— "Equal rights to all, special privileges to none"—challenged the operational maxims of both parties.[10]

For the Populists, the platform wasn't some Marxist historical critique but a morally grounded restatement of America's basic principles. The Populists believed they were channeling Jefferson's true intentions if not his exact teachings on government. Robber barons and their political handmaidens were threatening the way of life of the good people—the "producers," in their terminology—and using laissez-faire theories to defend their power. So in keeping with the maxim "Don't bring a knife to a gunfight," the Populists fought back on the strength of the people acting through an enhanced federal government. As Eric Goldman explains, the Populists looked to the Interstate Commerce Act and Sherman Antitrust Acts as models for how government could control the economy for the benefit of the people and break up concentrated economic power that threatened their way of life.[11]

Beyond the general principle of government power counterbalancing corporate power, the Populists' original platform laid out ten "sentiments" of the Omaha convention that became mainstays in progressive battles over the next forty years. Specific economic reforms included the graduated income tax, the eight-hour workday, pensions for soldiers, and a ban on corporate subsidies. Political reforms such as the secret ballot, the initiative and referendum process, direct elections of senators, and limited terms for president and vice president were also put forth. There were also more radical sentiments, including the nationalization of railroads and telegraph service, which signaled the severe distrust of the rail and utility barons and their political allies at the time.

In looking back, it is clear there were obvious downsides to populism, especially its nativist strand and anti-immigrant and anti-Semitic rhetoric. As Hofstadter argues, populist demagogues often derided the immorality of immigrants in the big cities and used terms such as "the international gold ring"—a clear anti-Semitic reference at the time—to criticize economic elites.[12] But these xenophobic attitudes were not uniform, however, and the Populists are credited with the first attempt at forging a genuinely biracial coalition of poor whites and blacks. As with much of American history, the Populists' actions in this regard frequently fell short of their expressions of racial equality but their defense of political and economic rights for blacks as part of common advancement for all farmers and laborers was well ahead of its time.[13]

The Populist movement may have kick-started a shift in political thinking in the United States, but as a political force it wasn't particularly long-lasting. The Populist Party won nearly 9 percent of the total vote and four states in the 1892 election—the strongest showing of any third party since the creation of the Republicans—and many Populist legislators were elected at the state and federal level. But serious infighting and bickering among the decentralized coalition of alliances from different regions plagued the Populists. Their ideas were ultimately absorbed by later reformers and presented in a more accommodating if no less challenging rhetorical form.

By 1896, the Populists joined forces with the Democrats in nominating William Jennings Bryan as their presidential candidate. As historian Michael Kazin argues in his biography, A Godly Hero, Bryan ("borrowing equally from Jefferson and Jesus") perhaps best captured the reformers' moral desire for change and their political desire to bring together the downtrodden into a powerful electoral coalition to pass legislative reforms to help farmers and laborers.[14] Bryan's first presidential run is heavily associated with "free silver" and agrarian concerns, but like the Populists, his policy platform previewed a number of specific ideas that would later become core progressive accomplishments.[15]

Although he failed to capture the presidency on three separate occasions, Bryan was a beloved leader and spectacular orator who dramatically transformed the Democratic Party from its small-government roots into a political force that believed in strong government willing to take on monopolies and privileged interests and to intervene on behalf of society's less influential groups.

As Kazin highlights, Bryan's famous speech at the Chicago Democratic convention concisely captured the emerging progressive position on government: "There are two ideas of government. There are those who believe that, if you will only legislate to make the well-to-do prosperous, their prosperity will leak through on those below. The Democratic idea, however, has been that if you legislate to make the masses prosperous, their prosperity will find its way up through every class which rests upon them."[16] These exact sentiments, used by progressives against Ronald Reagan's "trickle-down economics" in the 1980s, are quite similar to the economic positions of nearly every Democratic presidential aspirant in 2008.

It's difficult to overlook the importance of Bryan's strong evangelical faith in shaping his opinions about how government should help farmers and the working class. Progressivism is not your typical ideology built on immutable principles and deductive theories, but Progressives throughout history have relied on "eternal truths" to defend their ideas and ensure that the economy serves the people.

The principles embodied in the Declaration of Independence were one source of truth, and Christianity was another.

The Social Gospel movement and the rise of Catholic social justice work were critical developments behind the progressive impulse for economic fairness and justice. Personal faith and beliefs that the social teachings of Christ demanded action in this world drove many reformers to rise up and challenge the laissez-faire attitudes of the late nineteenth century. In *Progress and Poverty*, Henry George lambasted what today we would call the "prosperity gospel," arguing that conservative religion allowed the "rich Christian to bend on Sundays in a nicely upholstered pew . . . without any feeling of responsibility for the squalid misery that is festering but a square away."

Currently enjoying a modern renaissance among liberal Protestants and faithful progressives more generally, Walter Rauschenbusch's 1907 classic, *Christianity and the Social Crisis*, laid down the basic tenets of faith-based progressivism and offered a compelling argument for the social application of the Gospels. Like *Progress and Poverty* (Rauschenbusch claimed he was directly inspired by George and the single-tax activism of the 1880s), *Christianity and the Social Crisis* was immensely influential on future progressive movements and was an early influence on Martin Luther King, Jr. as he shaped his own theological and political thinking prior to the civil rights movement.

Rauschenbusch structured his book to make three major arguments that later came to embody basic Social Gospel thinking. First, in his historical chapters he stressed how "the essential purpose of Christianity was to transform human society into the kingdom of God by regenerating all human relations and reconstituting them in accordance with the will of God." His purpose was to show people how Christian teachings and the prophetic tradition of the Hebrew Bible could be put to use to foment social change during a period of want and suffering: "If anyone holds that religion is essentially ritual and sacramental; or that it is purely personal; or that God is on the side of the rich; or that social interest is likely to lead preachers astray; he must prove his case with his eye on the Hebrew prophets, and the burden of proof is with him."[17]

Second, like George and others before him, Rauschenbusch decried what he called the "present crisis" wrought by the industrial revolution and the rise of modern capitalism. But he upped the ante substantially by maintaining that Christian civilization could no longer withstand the injustices of contemporary times—inequality, poverty, physical deprivation and hunger, worker abuses. His solution was that desperate times required genuine moral leadership:

> If there are statesmen, prophets, and apostles who set truth and justice above selfish advancement; if their call finds a response in the great body of the people; if a new tide of religious faith and moral enthusiasm creates new standards of duty and a new capacity for self-sacrifice; if the strong learn to direct their love of power to the uplifting of the people and see the highest self-assertion in self-sacrifice— then the entrenchments of vested wrong will melt away; the stifled energy of the people will leap forward; the atrophied members of the social body will be filled with a fresh flow of blood; and a regenerate nation will look with the eyes of youth across the fields of the future.[18]

Third, Rauschenbusch argued that trying to turn back the clock on economic change was fruitless and that the primary goal of the Church should be to shape this change for the benefit of humanity.

To achieve the humanizing of capitalism, he encouraged more direct action like the settlement houses, he supported the organizing and solidarity of the labor movement, and he promoted the Christian volunteerism of preachers and groups such as the YMCA and the Salvation Army. Above all, however, Rauschenbusch counseled people to put their theological principles to work personally by adding "spiritual power along with the existing and natural relations of men to direct them to truer ends and govern them by higher motives."

Jane Addams and the world-famous Hull-House settlement she founded in the Nineteenth Ward of Chicago in 1889 represent one of the most direct applications of Social Gospel teachings at the time. Addams grew up in a well-to-do Quaker family and eventually was baptized as a Presbyterian. Her Christianity was very much focused on social action and the amelioration of sins and hardship on earth— a stance wholly consistent with humanitarian Social Gospel teachings.

Her social conscience steadily grew after trips to East London and other distressed areas, and she decided that her life's mission would be bringing education, opportunity, and citizenship to working-class and immigrant families on the South Side of Chicago. As Jean Bethke Elshtain argues in her biography of Addams, the Hull-House settlement—far from being charity or direct philanthropy—was designed as the embodiment of the Christian desire "to share the lives of the poor" and to build communal public spaces for people to learn and thrive and break down artificial barriers between classes and ethnicities.[19] Never once locking its doors, Hull-House offered poor families direct services such as baths, nurseries, kindergarten, and legal support; it provided the neighborhood with an inspiring place to study, organize, and discuss ideas; it had a wildly popular art gallery and offered math and social classes.[20]

Just as *Christianity and the Social Crisis* and the settlement movement represented the intersection of faith and progressive activism

for liberal Protestants, Pope Leo XIII's 1891 encyclical, *Rerum No-varum*, served as the intellectual basis for social activism for future American Catholics.* The Pope's statement on capital and labor sought to find a humane path for capitalism that respected workers and avoided the extremes of both socialism and laissez-faire conservatism. *Rerum Novarum* affirmed the right of state intervention on behalf of citizens, endorsed unionization, and affirmed property rights. Although it did not have the immediate impact in terms of Catholic activism that other Social Gospel texts and preaching had among evangelical Protestants, it did serve as the basis for generations of Catholic social justice reform and today is recognized as marking the new path for the Church's social doctrine.[21]

It is worth mentioning at this point that many of these early reformers, and later more famous ones such as FDR, were frequently accused by conservatives of being "socialists." There is no question that socialism and socialist ideas were swirling around America at this point and that a number of reformers shared socialists' broad critique of industrial capitalism and corrupted politics, if not their more radical prescriptions. Frustration with American capitalism at this time was shared by just about everyone except those making the big fortunes.

But it's important to note that progressives were not socialists and socialists were not progressives. The middle-class supporters of Teddy Roosevelt at the first Progressive Party convention in 1912

---

*The religiously inspired activism of Bryan, Rauschenbusch, and the settlement workers did not always fit with the desires of Catholic reformers. This was particularly true on the issue of prohibition, with the mostly southern and rural Protestants in the "dry" movement in conflict with the strong Catholic "wet" opposition concentrated among ethnic Germans and Irish. Prohibition, of course, did little for the country except to earn Al Capone a permanent place in Chicago history. Little wonder one of FDR's first acts was to repeal the ban on liquor in 1933.

were as interested in preventing socialism from taking hold in this country as they were in trying to keep big corporations in check.

Many progressive reformers viewed the class-based arguments of socialism as a European mentality unfit for American society with its non-feudal background and its long-standing commitment to individual liberty. In turn, many socialists believed that progressives were too moderate and accommodating of business. Many progressives preferred breaking up concentrated economic power and trusts before they got too big, whereas many socialists were content letting the private economy consolidate and then eventually having the state take over these big monopolies. This was alien thinking to American progressives rooted in the civic republicanism of Thomas Jefferson. Similarly, as Jean Bethke Elshtain highlights, progressives such as Jane Addams rejected socialism as a dogmatic and "secular" creed that failed to recognize the many important sources of reform spirit.[22] Reformers like Henry George fretted that socialist involvement in their movements was destructive and doctrinaire and left a taint that ruined their ability to build a broader base of support.

Some reformers, including the Populists and Bryan, proposed municipal ownership of utilities or nationalization of the railroads, but they argued these positions along Jeffersonian lines—challenging the big trusts to restore the ability of the little guy to compete. Their biggest concern was eradicating "special privileges" that certain companies had in their relationships with government. They had no interest in "nationalizing the means of production." They wanted farmers and workers to have more control over their livelihoods and future, not less. Similarly, the "gas and water socialism" of many big-city mayors was focused on practical needs such as sanitation and affordable transportation, not revolutionary action. Today's city waterworks and public transportation systems, along with city efforts to expand broadband access to their citizens, grew from this legacy.

Eugene Debs—who eventually captured 6 percent of the national vote running as the Socialist Party candidate in 1912 against two progressives, Teddy Roosevelt and Woodrow Wilson—thought of himself mostly as a trade unionist. He despised violence and identified more with Abraham Lincoln and America's democratic heritage than with the abstract theories and creeds that animated many socialists.[23]

In the end, it's clear that progressivism writ large was a distinctly American answer (the original "third way") to two ideological extremes of the time—socialism on the left and "survival-of-the-fittest" conservatism on the right. As a homegrown movement rather than a European import, American progressivism had far greater influence and many more accomplishments in politics than did socialism.

When you put all of these interesting characters and books and ideas together, what you get is a picture of early progressivism grounded in moral and political advocacy on behalf of those who lack power, money, and privilege in society. The impulse for these reform efforts arose from moral springs and long-standing beliefs about the nation's status as a land of freedom and autonomy rather than a class-based society rife with corruption and inequality. Some of the ideas were sound and remained influential in politics. Others were a bit too odd or radical to have long-lasting effects.

But all of them had the singular focus of trying to get a grip on economic changes that were undermining their belief in America as a land of opportunity and self-sufficiency. The primary goal of early progressives was to ensure that the economy worked for people, not the other way around. Their beliefs were not based on abstract ideas or philosophical treatises. Rather, they were built on practical experience and personal faith, a desire to fix real problems in the economy and to ensure that America's founding ideals were upheld.

CHAPTER 2

LESSON TWO

Progressives Believe in the Common Good, and a Government That Offers a Hand Up

The next important lesson I take from progressive history comes out of the explosion of legislative and executive actions at the city, state, and federal levels in the early twentieth century.

The early reformers—such as George, Donnelly, Bryan, Rauschenbusch, and others in various worker and farmer alliances—were more effective as moral agitators than as practitioners or government leaders. Notably, legions of progressive politicians including Teddy Roosevelt and Woodrow Wilson were initially skeptical and outright hostile to their emphatic calls for reform. As historian George Mowry explains, many of the most accomplished progressive reformers of the twentieth century on both the Republican and Democratic sides were considered outright conservatives in the 1890s.[1] During their mayoral battle in 1886, a young Roosevelt harshly criticized Henry George as a fanatic filled with crazy theories. Woodrow Wilson supported the "Gold Democratic" challenge to Bryan in 1896 and 1900. Even Robert "Fighting Bob" La Follette—the quintessential progressive—did not move away from the "regular Republicans" to support reform legislation in earnest until after he became governor of Wisconsin in 1901.

But TR and other progressive leaders would not have succeeded without the pioneering ideas and activism of these early agitators. People such as Henry George and the Populists brought to light the issues of poverty, squalor, corporate corruption, and lack of opportunity that drove more mainstream reformers to legislative action. By 1912, TR was trumpeting many of their ideas and actual proposals as the Progressive Party candidate for president while Woodrow Wilson was doing the same for the Democrats.

It's also clear, however, that much of the vision coming out of the Populist era would have languished without the broader-based, more mainstream and middle-class effort to help translate these ideas into the accomplishments of the Progressive and New Deal eras. As Teddy Roosevelt stated in his famous speech in Osawatomie, Kansas, "We must have—I believe we have already—a genuine and permanent moral awakening, without which no wisdom of legislation or administration really means anything; and, on the other hand, we must try to secure the social and economic legislation without which any improvement due to purely moral agitation is necessarily evanescent."[2]

Put another way, the single tax and free coinage of silver at a sixteen-to-one ratio with gold weren't exactly going to cut it as practical solutions to economic problems. Putting the moral vision of the Populists into concrete action, progressives created the graduated income and inheritance taxes and eventually established the Federal Reserve System to handle monetary issues (and which, in an ironic twist of its purpose as a lender of last resort to regulated banks, was recently used by conservatives in the Bush administration to help bail out Bear Stearns for making bad investments in mortgage-backed securities).

While their ideas were not always harmonious—and populist and progressive leaders did not always get along—their efforts were mutually reinforcing and helped to create a strong legacy of social improvements and strong government. Above all, this new political

movement focused its energy on turning government—once the bo-
geyman of democrats inspired by Jefferson—into a progressive force
for positive change, capable of improving the lives of citizens and promoting interests beyond those of the big trusts and robber barons.
This creation of socially oriented, empirically based government with
strong executive power took off from city halls to governors' mansions
and on to the White House and Congress in the early 1900s.

As the Populists and Bryan Democrats were pushing mostly
agrarian claims forward in the nineties, reformers at the city and
state levels began to come together to fix the problems of growing
urbanization. By the turn of the century, this urban-based reform
sentiment was coalescing into the original Progressive era, a period
that historians date from roughly 1900 to 1920.

The problems of the cities were severe. As David Von Drehle
recounts vividly in his book on the Triangle shirtwaist factory fire in
1911, people were packed in dense and often filthy tenements; industrial work paid little for long hours and dangerous working conditions; newly arrived immigrants lacked education, skills, and
integration with their communities; and corruption was the norm.[3]
Crime, transportation, sewage, electricity, and public health issues
had all become major problems for cities.

Muckraking journalists and writers like Jacob Riis and Lincoln
Steffens did much to expose these urban ills and bring political corruption to light during this era. Although reformers had been active
for many years prior to the rise of the muckrakers, their crusading
journalism helped to drive previously passive or resistant middle-
class citizens into progressive action.

In an early example of the power of investigative journalism,
Jacob Riis's 1890 book, *How the Other Half Lives*, is credited with driv-
ing his friend Teddy Roosevelt (as police commissioner of New
York City) to close filthy and dangerous tenements.

Fearful that more radical ideas might be seen as the solution to problems, middle-class citizens began to recognize that something had to be done to correct the injustices of modern urban life. The old ways of corrupt political bosses doing the bidding of corrupt business elites in opposition to the needs of the mass of citizens could no longer hold.

McClure's magazine—which was founded by Knox College classmates grounded in my alma mater's progressive tradition, and which later produced *New York Times* editor in chief John Huston Finley—published Lincoln Steffens's article "Tweed Days in St. Louis" in 1902, continuing the trend of exposing the cities' faults and announcing the birth of "muckraking" journalism (although the term itself was taken from a speech given later by Teddy Roosevelt).[4] Describing St. Louis in terms that would make modern-day scoundrels like Jack Abramoff blush, Steffens lambasted the business and political elites as the source of the decline of a once vibrant town:

Along about 1890, public franchises and privileges were sought, not only for legitimate profit and common convenience, but for loot. Taking but slight and always selfish interest in the public councils, the big men misused politics. The riffraff, catching the smell of corruption, rushed into the Municipal Assembly, drove out the remaining respectable men, and sold the city—its streets, its wharves, its markets, and all that it had—to the now greedy business men and bribers. In other words, when the leading men began to devour their own city, the herd rushed into the trough and fed also.

So gradually has this occurred that these same citizens hardly realize it. Go to St. Louis and you will find the habit of civic pride in them; they still boast ... But a change occurred. Public spirit became private spirit, public enterprise became private greed.[5]

Steffens's piece on St. Louis made him and the city's top reformer, city attorney Joseph "Holy Joe" Folk, famous across the land. It exposed the bribery of top business and political bosses such as Ed Butler and the effects of wholesale corruption on the workings of the city. Folk went on to prosecute the bosses and break up corrupt forces throughout the city and was later elected governor of Missouri on a reform platform.

Along with Ida Tarbell, who wrote a series exposing the underbelly of the Standard Oil Company, and Ray Stannard Baker, who wrote about racial issues and was a close confidant of Woodrow Wilson in later years, Steffens and other muckrakers brought the concerns of earlier reformers to a larger audience increasingly open to the ideas of progressivism. Their methods were factual reporting, the use of "shame" (as Steffens described it) to spark action, and a moral certitude about right and wrong—common progressive traits. Although most of the muckrakers disdained orthodox religion, many were imbued with a deep moral sense grounded in the Gospels and the early prophets. Justin Kaplan, in his biography of Lincoln Steffens, explains, "The muckrakers yearned to find Christian solutions to social problems and believed in the practical utility of the Golden Rule."[6]

In addition to exposing the dark side of American life, Steffens and other muckrakers also focused on successful reformers in the cities and states and challenged the notion that leaders such as Bob La Follette and Teddy Roosevelt were "demagogues" or "radicals" as the conservative business class often claimed. After his series on the cities, Steffens concluded, "[W]henever a man in public life was called a demagogue, there was something good about him, something dangerous to the system. And that since the plutogogues could not fasten any crime on him they fell back on the all-sufficient charge that he was a demagogue."[7]

The political and social crisis in America's cities was compounded by the lack of municipal control and massive amounts of graft and corruption at the state legislative level. Progressive reformers successfully challenged this corruption and created home-rule laws, city managers, and commissions to allow cities to experiment with solutions to their problems and keep corruption at bay. Teddy Roosevelt's fame as a reformer increased dramatically after his assault on the notoriously corrupt New York City police department and through his later work as governor on conservation, education, and corporate taxation.

Progressive mayors sprouted up across the country to support workers, provide social services for the indigent, set decent work standards, and challenge excessive corporate power, particularly among utility monopolies. "Good government" became the mantra of progressives trying to clean up the machine politics and corporate corruption of city services.

One of the more interesting progressive mayors, recounted in George Mowry's overview of the era, was Sam "Golden Rule" Jones of Toledo, Ohio. Like many of his predecessors I have already described, Jones's progressivism was grounded in his personal experience and Christian ethics. An immigrant who started his career in the oil industry in Pennsylvania, Jones eventually made a fortune through his own oil equipment company. His nickname comes from his "Golden Rule" philosophy that guided his own business practices—a model of humane treatment to workers with decent wages, an eight-hour workday, profit sharing, disability coverage, and paid vacations. For Jones, as long as his workers did their part and treated others decently, he would do the same for them.

As with many other leading progressives that emerged during this time, Jones was elected mayor as the Republican Party candidate in 1897 but later rejected his party bosses and embarked on an impressive string of forward-looking actions to improve life for residents in Toledo. Facing down fierce denunciations from the local business community, "Golden Rule" Jones died in office in 1904 with a legacy that included free kindergarten and night schools, a minimum wage and eight-hour day for city workers, housing for the homeless, and municipal parks.[8]

What "Golden Rule" Jones and others did for cities, governors such as Robert La Follette of Wisconsin and Albert Cummins of Iowa did for the states.

Perhaps one of the most acclaimed and widely respected progressives throughout history, Bob La Follette represented the progressive spirit in total. As David Thelen describes, La Follette was a man of humble, rural origins widely admired for his convictions and honesty.[9] He deplored corruption whether it occurred in government or in party machines. He believed ardently in standing on the side of the "common man" against business interests that exploited his labor and livelihood. He believed that government should be a force for good and the public welfare. As the *Milwaukee Journal* explained in 1930, La Follette's progressive spirit was a fighting one, confident and infectious to those who participated:

> [La Follette] dramatize[d] politics. Progressives are engaged in a gigantic struggle, staged before their own eyes in words and scenes of convincing power. Their leaders are warriors. Their cause is the cause of the people. . . . Speakers emphasize the state's social obligations—to all who work, to dependents, to those harshly dealt with by the social order. To the progressives politics has become an epic, in which great

figures move from triumph to triumph—and the progressive voter sees himself as sharing in every triumph.[10]

Bob La Follette believed that the essence of the Progressive movement was to "uphold the fundamental principles of representative government" and put forth "the hopes and desires of millions of common men and women who are willing to fight for their ideals, to take defeat if necessary, and still go on fighting."[11]

La Follette took this fighting spirit first to the Republican Party machine that controlled the nominating process and then to the corporate interests that controlled the state of Wisconsin. La Follette helped to pass the first direct primary legislation in the nation and went on to promote the "Wisconsin idea"—reform principles grounded in empirical research about good government and social benefits for citizens carried out in conjunction with social scientists and other academics from the University of Wisconsin. In *The American Mind*, Henry Steele Commager describes the "Wisconsin idea" and La Follette's governing theory as follows: "His approach to every problem was practical and pragmatic rather than moral or theoretical. It consisted of investigation, the collection of statistics, the application of scientific principles by impartial boards and commissions, and the encouragement of what Lester Ward had called 'social invention.'"[12] La Follette's experiments in governance led Teddy Roosevelt to extol Wisconsin as "an experimental laboratory of wise governmental action in aid of social and industrial justice"—an idea embraced by progressives to this day in their battles for expanded health care, school reform, crime reduction, and living wage legislation in the states.[13]

In addition to the direct primary law, La Follette passed legislation to control the railroads, increase taxation on corporations, encourage civil service reforms to limit patronage, start conservation measures, and control state banks, as Alice Honeywell highlights.[14] As both a governor and a U.S. senator, La Follette was a vocal champion for numerous progressive causes, including workers' compensation, the minimum wage, conservation, regulation of business, voting rights for women, and the direct election of senators.

In his autobiography, La Follette recounts one of the more telling episodes of progressive history, highlighting how reformers placed a premium on doing what is right regardless of political expediency or partisanship.

Traveling through Wisconsin, William Jennings Bryan called Governor La Follette to ask him how his legislation was coming along. La Follette said his pending railroad bill was in jeopardy and asked "Colonel Bryan" to help out. Bryan agreed, argued vehemently for La Follette's reforms before the legislature, and made the point that "he was not afraid of Republicans stealing Democratic thunder; that he would be willing to leave all the good Democratic propositions that had ever been advanced out on the porch over night if only the Republicans would steal them and enact them into law."[15]

La Follette also recounts how Bryan refused to campaign against him in the 1902 elections, with Bryan stating to him, "I am tremendously interested in what you are doing in Wisconsin and I want to see you succeed. It is more important in its example to the country than any triumph of the Democratic Party in that state. I want to see you get a state primary. I want to see you carry out your taxation propositions. I want to see you win out in your contest with the corporations."[16]

Another midwestern Republican governor and Senator, Albert Cummins of Iowa, aided La Follette's progressive crusade. Cummins, like La Follette, beat back the Republican machine and was elected on an "anti-monopoly, anti-railroad, low tariff platform."[17] Cummins's inaugural address, recounted by Benjamin Gue, concisely

summarized progressive opinion about the anti-democratic nature of
corporate political dominance and lobbying:

> Wealth gives to him who owns or controls it power for
> great good and great evil; it gives him power to endow
> schools, found libraries, and relieve want; but it also gives
> him power to seduce and coerce his fellow men, and this
> power should be most jealously scrutinized. Incorporated
> wealth has many rights; but it should always be remem-
> bered that among these is not the right to vote. Corpora-
> tions have, and ought to have many privileges; but among
> them is not the right to sit in political conventions or oc-
> cupy seats in legislative chambers.[18]

In looking at these actions at the local and state level, it is important to remember that at its root, progressivism is a bottom-up
creed built on ethical foundations and practical actions focused on
the needs of real people. Progressives pursued political reforms
such as the initiative and direct primary not through analysis of
democratic theory, but because there was no way to get around the
corporate brokers and government powers who controlled the political process. Progressives fought for regulation and oversight of
the railroads not because of some grand idea about public ownership but because the rail trusts gave big customers special rates
and rebates. They fought for social benefits for the poor and public improvements such as parks and schools not to fulfill some
elaborate social philosophy but because the cities could no longer
tolerate the inhumane conditions under which many of their residents lived.

Notwithstanding all the reform activity at the city and state levels, it became clear to progressives that reforms could no longer be

piecemeal and regional. Many of the problems in American life were national—challenging the trusts, social welfare legislation, land and resource conservation—and required a force that could effectively respond across the country and with real leverage.

The presidencies of Theodore Roosevelt, Woodrow Wilson, and Franklin Roosevelt exemplify the progressive tradition of enhancing national power for the betterment of individuals and society. Although each was criticized in some capacity by other progressives at the time for falling short of the reform ideal—particularly Woodrow Wilson for his suppression of civil liberties during World War I— each in his own way advanced the cause of reform for a wide segment of Americans. Their actions matter greatly for understanding the progressive story.

At the same time, I do not want to overstate the "great man" theory of change by focusing only on the accomplishment of former presidents. There is no question that their legislative accomplishments would have been impossible without the decades of activism and movement building by progressives from all walks of life.

Each of these leaders put forth powerful arguments for reform; each challenged special privilege; each increased the reach of executive authority to manage the economy more effectively; and each leader promoted legislation to increase the opportunity of Americans and address the excesses of capitalism. Countless volumes of history and interpretation exist on these presidents, so I will just briefly cover what I think are some of their more important contributions to progressivism.

Teddy Roosevelt is held up in many circles as the archetypal progressive, although there was considerable contemporary debate about his progressive bona fides. From my point of view, Teddy Roosevelt embodied both the pugnacious and pragmatic elements of the progressive spirit, and through his personal popularity and presidential actions and rhetoric, he did as much as anyone in history to bring the "applied idealism" of progressivism to a wider public.

Roosevelt was an upper-class reformer who started off conservative and steadily moved left. He is famously, and in a somewhat exaggerated fashion, referred to as a "trust-buster" who called out the "malefactors of great wealth." (As TR biographer Henry Pringle notes, Roosevelt "started only twenty-five proceedings leading to indictments under the Sherman [Antitrust] Act, while [the business-friendly] Taft began forty-five.")[19] His regulatory legacy includes the Pure Food and Drug Act, which set up permanent testing of the food supply and prescriptions for certain medicines, and numerous executive actions protecting millions of acres of public lands and waterways.

The end of Roosevelt's second term was marked by increasingly progressive ideas about corporate regulation, conservation, and the importance of using government for the public good. TR articulated a coherent explanation of progressive thought with his new nationalist vision of enhanced federal government authority to regulate corporations and streamline the economy. He was a renegade Republican who broke with his handpicked successor, William Howard Taft, and challenged the leading progressive icon at the time, Robert La Follette, to run as the presidential candidate of the first Progressive Party, one of the most successful third parties in history.

To better understand the impact of TR's program on America, it is useful to focus on what I think are two of his more important and long-lasting contributions to progressivism—his conservation efforts and his ideas about government and the economy expressed in the "New Nationalism" and the platform of the Progressive Party.

If you've ever taken a family trip to the Grand Canyon or any one of the 150 national forests, 51 bird reserves, 18 national monuments, or 5 national parks set aside in the early 1900s, you can thank Teddy Roosevelt and his progressive ideas on land use.[20] There's no better way to assess the direct impact of progressive ideas on society than to examine TR's conservation legacy and his protection of more than 230 million acres of public lands.

An ardent outdoorsman and nature lover, Roosevelt established a far-reaching federal agenda to protect America's natural resources and public lands for recreation and smart commercial use. This legacy of stewardship and conservation—carried out with esteemed conservationist Gifford Pinchot as director of the U.S. Forest Service—became the blueprint for all future progressive environmental actions.

From the beginning of his presidency in 1901, sustainable use of natural resources was a top priority for Roosevelt's administration.* TR implored people to put aside prior misconceptions about the unlimited quantity and quality of America's resources and to focus instead on how best to reverse the flagrant misuse of the nation's land, timber, coal, and gas supplies and the ongoing degradation of its waterways.

Prior to the Newlands Reclamation Act of 1902, the creation of the United States Forest Service in 1905, and the passage of the Antiquities Act in 1906, the notion that America's resources were to be harnessed for the national good and protected from overuse was anathema to the legions of mining, timber, and power companies seeking to exploit these riches. For decades, America's natural bounty was open game for expropriation by private interests.

In 1908, addressing the first gathering of the nation's governors

---

*TR and Gifford Pinchot used the term "wise use" to describe their policies. The term was expropriated by Ronald Reagan's interior secretary, James Watt, and anti-environmentalist Ron Arnold, to fight regulation and defend the interests of the extraction industry.

in an address entitled "Conservation as a National Duty," Roosevelt explained his administration's theory of public resource use:

> We are coming to recognize as never before the right of the Nation to guard its own future in the essential matter of natural resources. In the past we have admitted the right of the individual to injure the future of the Republic for his own present profit. In fact there has been a good deal of a demand for unrestricted individualism, for the right of the individual to injure the future of all of us for his own temporary and immediate profit. The time has come for a change. As a people we have the right and the duty, second to none other but the right and duty of obeying the moral law, of requiring and doing justice, to protect ourselves and our children against the wasteful development of our natural resources, whether that waste is caused by the actual destruction of such resources or by making them impossible of development hereafter. . . . Such a policy will preserve soil, forests, water power as a heritage for the children and the children's children of the men and women of this generation; for any enactment that provides for the wise utilization of the forests, whether in public or private ownership, and for the conservation of the water resources of the country, must necessarily be legislation that will promote both private and public welfare; for flood prevention, water-power development, preservation of the soil, and improvement of navigable rivers are all promoted by such a policy of forest conservation.[21]

Roosevelt directed the gathering governors to "formulate a national philosophy of conservation based on efficient use of finite resources and scientific management of renewable ones," and, with their consent, proceeded to create the National Conservation Commission to implement this philosophy, along with commissions on rural living and inland waterways. In less than two years, forty-four states had created their own conservation commissions.[22] As Edmund Morris shows, Roosevelt's environmental vision extended beyond America—he is credited with creating the first hemispheric alliance with Canada and Mexico to address ecological concerns on a global basis.[23]

Not surprisingly, Roosevelt faced fierce opposition to his conservation agenda, primarily from mining, timber, and ranching interests and voters in the West. These interests, with their political allies in Congress, believed that America's natural resources were rightfully theirs to exploit however they saw fit. These natural resource interests drew on the same laissez-faire doctrine and rhetoric about property rights that other conservatives had used to beat back unions, stop social legislation, and prevent public interest regulation.

Roosevelt viewed conservation not just as a means for protection but also as a theory of economic development and a microcosm of what he called "national efficiency." TR spelled out this larger theory of efficiency in his post-presidency speech "The New Nationalism," delivered in Osawatomie, Kansas, in 1910. This speech offers one of the more easily digestible and coherent explanations of progressive thought available.

Although Roosevelt had previewed many of these themes late in his second term, this particular speech appears to be heavily informed by his interpretation of Herbert Croly's influential book *The Promise of American Life*, first published in 1909. Historians disagree about the extent to which Roosevelt was influenced by Croly and vice versa, but as Michael McGerr argues, the modern consensus seems to be that they reached their complementary ideas about the role of the state independent of each other.[24]

Croly's central thesis nicely encapsulates the gathering thought in progressive circles: primarily that the "American promise"—the belief that future life will be better for individuals and America as a whole—could no longer be fulfilled unless Americans replaced the small-government individualism of Jefferson with a new American nationalism (associated with Hamiltonian federalism) that would harness the power of the state to regulate big business, labor, agriculture, and other aspects of the economy for the national interest and extend social benefits to the working classes. In contrast to the populist and early progressive reformers he criticized, Croly accepted the combination of business interests as unavoidable and beneficial, assuming they were checked by an equally powerful government and driven toward activity that would benefit both individuals and society as a whole.

Unlike Croly's book, however, TR's New Nationalism speech does not fully reject progressives' Jeffersonian heritage and manages to fuse all of the existing progressive goals into a coherent vision based on eliminating special privilege, restoring individual opportunity, and building an effective national government focused on the common good. With this speech, Roosevelt essentially created a modern theory of checks and balances (similar in spirit if not form to James Madison's defense of checks and balances and separation of powers in the Constitution) to manage the increasingly complex relationships among business, unions, individuals, and government.

Roosevelt began his Osawatomie speech outlining the challenges of the day and connecting them to the battles of Abraham Lincoln: "Exactly as the special interests of cotton and slavery threatened our political integrity before the Civil War, so now the great special business interests too often control and corrupt the men and methods of government for their own profit." He called for political reforms to end the corrupt influence of business by banning corporate donations, eliminating public franchises, holding corporate leaders accountable for illegal actions, establishing oversight of interstate businesses, and creating tariff commissions.

Roosevelt then expressed the progressive belief in equality of opportunity and the need to ensure that rising wealth is not inimical to common needs. "The man who wrongly holds that every human right is secondary to his profit must now give way to the advocate of human welfare, who rightly maintains that every man holds his property subject to the general right of the community to regulate its use to whatever degree the public welfare may require it." Roosevelt also said the government has the right to regulate labor and that regulation should not be punitive: "The fundamental thing to do for every man is to give him a chance to reach a place in life in which he will make the greatest possible contribution to the public welfare. Understand what I say there. Give him a chance, not push him up if he will not be pushed. Help any man who stumbles; if he lies down, it is a poor job to try to carry him; but if he is a worthy man, try your best to see that he gets a chance to show the worth that is in him."

Echoing the civic republican ideals of Jefferson (and perhaps anticipating his distant cousin Franklin's ideas about freedom from want), Roosevelt claimed, "No man can be a good citizen unless he has a wage more than sufficient to cover the bare cost of living, and hours of labor short enough so after his day's work is done he will have time and energy to bear his share in the management of the community, to help in carrying the general load. We keep countless men from being good citizens by the conditions of life by which we surround them."

He then laid out a series of progressive social reforms to accomplish this new vision—workers' compensation, a ban on child labor and regulation of work for women, practical training in schools, sanitary conditions and workplace safety measures—and called on reformers to renounce violence as a means for human advancement.

In his formulation, the New Nationalism was not a call for overcentralization of power, but a spirit of "broad and far reaching nationalism where we work for what concerns our people as a whole," and the recognition that the "National Government belongs to the whole American people, and where the whole American people are interested, that interest can be guarded effectively only by the National Government." His goal was to "put the national need before sectional or personal advantage" through strong executive power "as the steward of the public welfare," a judiciary "interested primarily in human welfare rather than in property," and a legislature that represents "all the people rather than any one class or section of people."

Roosevelt wisely tempered this vision by saying government has a duty to protect property as well as human welfare and that "reformers should not bring upon the people economic ruin." But he challenged those who opposed reform to recognize that "ruin in its worst form is inevitable if our national life brings us nothing better than swollen fortunes for the few and the triumph in both politics and business of a sordid and selfish materialism."

In his final words from Kansas, Roosevelt talked about the importance of aligning good character with good laws, proclaiming, "The prime problem of our nation is to get the right type of good citizenship, and, to get it, we must have progress, and our public men must be genuinely progressive."

Roosevelt's speech truly captures the progressive spirit and project in clear terms. Like the populists and earlier social agitators, it provided a call for a moral awakening to challenge the problems of the day. It outlined the long-standing program of expanded governmental authority to promote the national interest and ensure equality of opportunity. Most of the themes from earlier and future progressive efforts are in this speech: political reforms to stop the influence of corrupt business, public interest regulations to harness the good parts of the emerging economy while ensuring health and workplace safety standards, social benefits for those left out of economic progress, a commitment to economic justice for the little guy, and a strong executive leading the charge in conjunction with a judiciary and legislature that are honest brokers and vessels of the people.

Roosevelt's attempts to appeal to both progressives and conservatives in this speech reflected a more immediate political need to bring together the warring factions within the Republican Party. By 1912, these divisions had grown intolerable, and the insurgents in the party, primarily the midwestern and western progressives, moved in a far more aggressive direction. The progressive faction at first turned to Bob La Follette—a consistent and strong voice for reform—to lead the charge against Taft. But many leading progressive voices believed La Follette could not defeat Taft and instead pushed Roosevelt into the battle.[25] After attempting to capture the Republican Party nomination in 1912, only to have it taken away by Taft and his allies, Roosevelt went on to carry the mantle of reform with Hiram Johnson, governor of California, as the nominees of the newly created Progressive Party.

As historian Arthur Link describes, the Progressive platform—like the Populist Party platform before it—defined the program for the next generation, eventually culminating in many of the New Deal successes in the 1930s.[26] Explaining the rationale for the new party in his opening address, "Confession of Faith," TR stated flatly:

> It seems to me, therefore, that the time is ripe, and over-ripe, for a genuine Progressive movement, nation-wide

and justice-loving, sprung from and responsible to the people themselves, and sundered by a great gulf from both of the old party organizations, while representing all that is best in the hopes, beliefs, and aspirations of the plain people who make up the immense majority of the rank and file of both the old parties.[27]

Embracing the vision of Jefferson and Lincoln "that the people are the masters of their Constitution," the Progressive platform called for some of the most far-reaching reforms ever put forth by a major national party: direct primaries; direct election of senators; the initiative, referendum, and recall; health and safety standards in the workplace; taxing authority over interstate commerce; prohibition of child labor; living wage; federal eight-hour day and six-day week; ban on convict labor; workers' compensation; unemployment and old-age insurance; expanded public education; investment in industrial research and development; tariff revision; conservation and waterways protection; women's suffrage; lobbyist reform; restrictions on labor injunctions; investment in roads and national highways; a graduated income tax and inheritance tax; fair treatment of immigrants; and federal oversight over investment and stock sales.

Throughout the 1912 campaign, Roosevelt pressed his New Nationalism themes and the social welfare aspects of the Progressive platform in explicit contrast to his Democratic competitor, Woodrow Wilson. Wilson, the somewhat conservative governor of New Jersey at the time, embraced the progressive spirit but built his vision on the ideas of Louis Brandeis, promoting what he called the "New Freedom"—a Jeffersonian vision of expanded federal authority to eliminate special privilege, break up monopolies, and restore competition.

Over time, many commentators would conclude that the New Nationalism and New Freedom were distinctions without substantial difference. But in the heat of the presidential battle, Wilson went so far as to categorize Roosevelt's social plans as "paternalistic" and a form of enslavement, while Roosevelt accused Wilson of promoting "rural Toryism" that supported laissez-faire.[28]

Wilson emerges in the historical literature as a somewhat contentious progressive leader, a reluctant reformer who drove important legislative accomplishments but equally suspect actions that challenged his progressive credentials. Wilson pushed to reduce tariffs and reform the banking and currency system through the creation of the Federal Reserve System. He also made a big concession to the New Nationalism idea of accepting but regulating business through his creation of the Federal Trade Commission (FTC). Wilson presided over major constitutional changes including the direct election of U.S. senators, the creation of the income tax, and women's suffrage. This domestic legacy, along with his influential efforts to construct a new international architecture (see chapter 4), is enough to earn Wilson a secure place among progressive reformers.

But as Arthur Link explains, many progressives bemoaned his early unwillingness to take on the child labor question or to push equal suffrage. They deplored his segregationist policies. Progressives later scratched their heads over his appointment of representatives of business and banking interests to the newly created Federal Reserve Board and FTC. When Wilson stated prematurely in 1914 that his New Freedom program had effectively completed the progressive mission of the previous two decades, Herbert Croly wrote in the *New Republic* that Wilson "had utterly misconceived the meaning and the task of American progressivism."[29]

Wilson's later years were particularly problematic for progressives. As Michael McGerr argues, Wilson's legacy of internationalism in world affairs is rightly praised, but his administration's propaganda efforts and clampdown on civil liberties during World War I eventually signaled the death knell of progressivism until the days of Franklin Roosevelt.[30]

From the Espionage Act and Sedition Act to the roundup of suspected radicals and the propaganda efforts of the Committee on Public Information, Wilson's war effort twisted the progressive project to support flagrantly anti-progressive propaganda and suppression efforts. As Geoffrey Stone recounts, government acts (based on the idea of not obstructing the recruitment and morale of soldiers) led to people being imprisoned for sending chain letters that called for peace or petitioning for draft reforms. Filmmaker Robert Goldstein was sent to prison for ten years for producing a movie about the American Revolution because—as the government argued—it attempted to foment insubordination by portraying Britain in a negative light.[31] Attorney General A. Mitchell Palmer, with the help of his young aide, J. Edgar Hoover, launched a series of raids that arrested more than six thousand suspected troublemakers during the Red Scare of 1919–1920—many of whom were guilty of nothing but being foreign-born.[32]

Although leading political voices such as La Follette and Jane Addams opposed these efforts, the participation of other known progressives and muckrakers offers a cautionary tale for how progressive belief in national goals can be taken too far. By aligning themselves so closely with Wilson, the majority of progressives may have helped to win the Great War, but they also lost part of their souls in the process by putting the national war project above individual liberty in too many cases.

As a direct result of the Wilson administration's clear over-reaching in the war effort, progressivism entered a period of reconsideration and reversal in the 1920s. As Paul Starr notes in his book *Freedom's Power*, the use of the term *liberal* began to increase around this time to distinguish new reforms from the progressive past and some of its perceived excesses (the term *liberal* had enjoyed much wider usage and understanding in Britain prior to this period).[33] It wasn't long before the successive Republican administrations of Warren Harding, Calvin Coolidge, and Herbert Hoover erased many of the progressive gains of the early twentieth century by "cutting the hated income tax, ignoring organized labor and the poor, and allowing big business to dominate federal regulatory agencies," as Starr explains.[34]

The return to laissez-faire did not last long, and by the end of the 1920s, the country was again mired in severe economic depression, with millions of able-bodied men and women out of work and a financial system on the brink of total collapse.

Just as economic turbulence sparked the earlier Populist revolt, the decline of the American economy in the early 1930s led to perhaps the most successful period of national progressive reform under Franklin Roosevelt. Without going into the detail the period demands, I'll finish up this lesson by briefly examining how FDR's political thought and experimentation offer critical insight into how progressives harnessed government for the benefit of the common good, thus avoiding the extremes of socialism and "survival-of-the-fittest" conservatism.

It's somewhat difficult today to imagine the bleak economic conditions in 1933, when FDR took office. According to historian Harold Faulkner, an estimated 13–17 million Americans were unemployed; agricultural products declined sharply in value; business output was well below normal; exports were down; and the banking system imploded as thousands of banks closed their doors.[35] Much as Wilson had mobilized the nation for world conflict, FDR harnessed the full force of governmental action to lead the nation out of depression and to create a political structure that could ensure economic stability and social protections from future shocks.

In his 1933 book, *Looking Forward*, FDR laid out a concise view of history and a set of values that explained his motives for change. He presented his progressive vision as a continuation of the original American "contract"—the right of self-government and the right to life, liberty, and the pursuit of happiness—created by Jefferson and updated by Teddy Roosevelt and Woodrow Wilson. Roosevelt proclaimed that the purpose of government "has always been whether individual men and women will have to serve some system of government or economics or whether a system of government and economics exists to serve individual men and women."[36]

As Arthur Schlesinger Jr. recounts, FDR drew on a range of philosophical ideas from old-line liberalism to Croly-style nationalism and Wilsonian New Freedom to design policies that would correct economic injustices while protecting individuals from excessive government interference.[37] He called for economic planning to avoid "the terrible cycle of prosperity crumbling into depression," and sought to update the contract with citizens to ensure that every man had "a right to make a comfortable living."[38]

His first inaugural address called for new controls on speculative banking and investment interests and new programs to "put people to work."[39] In the first three months of his administration—the famous Hundred Days—FDR signed into law fifteen major initiatives to save the American economy, including the Emergency Banking Act, the creation of the Civilian Conservation Corps, the abandonment of the gold standard, the Federal Emergency Relief Act, the Agricultural Adjustment Act, the Tennessee Valley Authority, the Securities Act, the Glass-Steagall Act (to implement banking regulations), and the National Industrial Recovery Act.[40] Soon afterward came massive programs to expand rural electrification and—through agencies such as the Civil Works Administration and the Works Progress Administration—public works projects that set up "39,000 new schools (70 percent of all new schools built during the 1930s), 2,500 new hospitals, 325 airports, and tens of thousands of smaller projects," according to Jonathan Alter in his recent book about the Hundred Days.[41]

Even with the courts stepping in to strike down his early New Deal legislation, Roosevelt pushed ahead with a second New Deal that included the creation of Social Security in 1935 and passage of the National Labor Relations Act, which formally recognized union organizing, collective bargaining, and strikes. Combined, FDR's actions in the 1930s solidified the aspirations of countless reformers dating back to the late nineteenth century and set the nation on the course of government support and intervention in the economy that remains to this day (despite attacks on this legacy by the new proponents of laissez-faire).

Although many economists and historians believe that it took World War II to lift America fully out of the Great Depression, few people discount Roosevelt's achievements in updating America's social contract to help the least fortunate among us. As Alter and others recount, FDR's moral mission was stated clearly in his second inaugural: "The test of our progress is not whether we add to the abundance of those who have much. It is whether we provide enough for those who have too little."[42] Progressives today are not only trying to protect FDR's legislative and economic achievements but are also finding modern ways to fulfill his vision for a more equitable and peaceful world order.

In State of the Union addresses delivered in 1941 and 1944,

FDR put forth two important intellectual frameworks that remain core values for modern progressives. His conception of the "Four Freedoms" necessary to guide global relations—freedom of speech and expression, freedom of religion, freedom from want, and freedom from fear—is a bedrock expression of liberal humanitarianism and later became the philosophical blueprint of the UN Declaration of Human Rights.

Similarly, FDR's call for a second Bill of Rights built on political measures to ensure economic advancement put forth an equally ambitious set of values designed to eradicate poverty and inequality on the domestic front. Roosevelt said the nation could not be "content, no matter how high that general standard of living may be, if some fraction of our people—whether it be one-third or one-fifth or one-tenth—is ill-fed, ill-clothed, ill-housed, and insecure," and expressly enumerated concrete economic rights, including:

The right to a useful and remunerative job in the industries or shops or farms or mines of the nation;

The right to earn enough to provide adequate food and clothing and recreation;

The right of every farmer to raise and sell his products at a return which will give him and his family a decent living;

The right of every businessman, large and small, to trade in an atmosphere of freedom from unfair competition and domination by monopolies at home or abroad;

The right of every family to a decent home;

The right to adequate medical care and the opportunity to achieve and enjoy good health;

The right to adequate protection from the economic fears of old age, sickness, accident, and unemployment;

The right to a good education.

While some of the specifics may seem dated, the basic principle that freedom requires economic opportunity and minimum measures of security—food, housing, medical care, old age protection—remains central to the progressive project of today. Modern commentators tend to dismiss the New Deal as a model for contemporary politics, but I believe that the ideals expressed by FDR in the Four Freedoms and the Economic Bill of Rights remain a high-water mark for progressivism and set the standards for all later reform efforts.

As Texas New Dealer Maury Maverick famously postulated, democracy is basically "liberty plus groceries." It may sound crude, but it's as good an explanation of progressive politics as anything I've heard.

CHAPTER 3

LESSON THREE

Progressives Hold That All People Are Equal in the Eyes of God and Under the Law

One glaring hole in the accomplishments of early progressives was their unwillingness or inability to challenge effectively the legacy of racism in American society. This sin dates back to Jefferson and other progressive forebears and is particularly vexing given progressive actions to break down class and gender barriers around the turn of the century. Fortunately, over time and with much prodding, progressives eventually aligned their actions with stated principles on human equality to become a dominant force for social tolerance and political and economic rights for all.

How did this transition occur? Building on the abolitionist and women's suffrage movements, the tide forever turned when the moral and political activism of the black community aligned with white liberals to shift the overall direction of the progressive project profoundly during the height of the civil rights movement from 1954 to 1965. The lesson here is that significant political change almost always comes from the bottom up, through persistent moral activism and the concrete action of brave citizens and their leaders standing up to injustice in all its forms.

Progressives had started to move toward a strong pro-civil-rights position in the aftermath of World War II, but it took the

Montgomery bus boycott, the sit-ins in Greensboro and other southern cities, the Freedom Rides, and the marches to drive passage of the "second emancipation" and secure the legacy of racial equality and opportunity. No longer would progressivism be a voice for the advancement of poor and middle-class whites only; it would become the creed for the advancement and equality of all people. As Paul Starr argues, the civil rights movement in turn became the model for all future progressive activism for the advancement of women, immigrants, gays and lesbians, and people with disabilities.[1]

Looking back on the Progressive and New Deal eras, the historical record is markedly negative in terms of support for racial justice. Many leading progressives either actively promoted segregation (as Woodrow Wilson did by introducing formal segregation into the executive branch during his presidency), held attitudes of racial superiority (as was the case with Teddy Roosevelt), or were sympathetic but not inclined to support African American equality due to political considerations and the need for southern votes (which is the leading explanation for many New Deal liberals). As George Mowry shows in his overview of the era, some progressives (particularly middle-class urban reformers) were anti-immigrant, anti-Catholic, and anti-Jewish—holding biases based on faulty assumptions about the role of immigrants in the corruption and poor sanitary conditions of the cities.[2]

One might chalk up these attitudes to the times or political reality. But given the stated principles of progressives, it is not incorrect or historically backward to say that many progressives were just plain wrong on a critical set of issues having to do with human dignity and equality. It's an important lesson that should chasten progressives to this day.

Within a framework of overall indifference or hostility toward black advancement during the era, there were prominent white voices that stood out for racial equality, including people such as Mary

Ovington, Jane Addams, and Lincoln Steffens, who joined W. E. B. Du Bois and other black leaders to found the National Association for the Advancement of Colored People (NAACP) in 1909. Addams later cast the lone vote to seat black southern delegations at the first Progressive Party convention in 1912.[3] Eleanor Roosevelt also provided a strong voice for racial justice during her husband's administration despite internal efforts to keep her quiet for fear of upsetting southern voters. FDR himself said that his Economic Bill of Rights should be accorded to all citizens regardless of "station, race or creed."

Looking back, it is not surprising that many of the early progressive voices for racial equality were also at the front lines of battles to secure full equality for women. Building on their experiences in the anti-slavery movement, Elizabeth Cady Stanton and Lucretia Mott pioneered the fight for women's rights at the Seneca Falls convention in 1848. In the spirit of the Declaration of Independence, Stanton's "Declaration of Sentiments" at the convention proclaimed that "all men and women are created equal" and went on to catalogue the numerous "injuries and usurpations on the part of man toward woman." At the top of the list of charges was, "He has never permitted her to exercise her inalienable right to the elective franchise."[4]

Out of the Seneca Falls convention and aftermath of the Civil War grew the women's suffrage movement, led by Stanton and Susan B. Anthony, the co-founders of the National Woman Suffrage Association, and Lucy Stone, co-founder of the American Woman Suffrage Association. Of all of the steps to ensure equality for women, none was more important to the early feminists than the right to vote, for pioneering feminists believed that only with a legitimate and binding political voice for women would other reforms be possible.[5]

The National Woman's Party (NWP) grew out of a political split between the two groups and led a more aggressive charge for suffrage, including a variety of marches, strikes, and pickets, to get across its message. The NWP staged a famous protest in front of the White House in 1917 to pressure Woodrow Wilson, a reluctant suffragist, to support a constitutional amendment. Eventually, these collective actions culminated in the passage of the Nineteenth Amendment (ratified in 1920), which guaranteed full voting rights for women.

About the same time the suffragists were pressing their case, W. E. B. Du Bois was making the argument for full equality and educational attainment for blacks. Du Bois's groundbreaking 1903 book, *The Souls of Black Folk*, presciently argued that the chief problem of the twentieth century would be the "color-line" and proceeded to lay out the ideals of black freedom and advancement that defined civil rights battles for decades to come.

Drawing on the principles of the Declaration of Independence (as did the early feminists), Du Bois explicitly rejected the idea that black Americans could succeed in a world defined by the "separate but equal" doctrine enshrined in the notorious *Plessy v. Ferguson* case of 1896. He also challenged the prevailing strategy of accommodation— "learn, work and earn the respect of the white man," as Eric Goldman describes it—associated with the leading black figure at the time, Booker T. Washington.[6]

Although Du Bois believed Washington was sincere in his efforts to promote acceptance of racial separatism as a means for relative peace and opportunity for blacks, he sharply criticized the theory for giving up three critical elements of black advancement: "political power . . . insistence on civil rights . . . [and the] higher education of Negro youth."[7] The implication of Washington's theory, according to Du Bois, was "that the South is justified in its present attitude toward the Negro because of the Negro's degradation; secondly, that the prime cause of the Negro's failure to rise more quickly is his wrong education in the past; and, thirdly, that his future rise depends primarily on his own efforts."

Du Bois brought together leading black intellectuals—what he called the "talented tenth"—to formalize a more aggressive approach to equal rights for blacks under the banner of the Niagara Movement, a civil rights organization founded by Du Bois and others. At the group's second conference in Harpers Ferry, West Virginia, Du Bois and his cohorts outlined a set of demands that would define civil rights activism for generations: full manhood suffrage, the end of discrimination in public accommodations, freedom to "walk, talk, and be with them that wish to be with us," laws enforced equally against rich and poor and enforcement of constitutional due process, and "real education" for blacks. The Niagara Movement stated that it would seek to get these demands met through nonviolent means including voting, "persistent, unceasing agitation," hard work, and "hammering the truth."[8]

The NAACP, coming out of the Niagara Movement, held its first conference on the anniversary of Abraham Lincoln's birthday, calling for a renewal of Lincoln's promise of freedom and equality for every citizen regardless of race. The NAACP launched its first legal proceeding the following year, defending a black farmhand convicted for unknowingly killing a policeman in self-defense after the officer broke into his home.[9] The NAACP went on to win numerous Supreme Court cases striking down legal segregation in housing, the military, and schools.

The cause of racial equality reached a boiling point in the aftermath of World War II. As Eleanor Roosevelt and others correctly argued during the war, the United States could not proclaim a moral victory over totalitarianism in Europe while condoning violent and discriminatory behavior at home.[10] By 1948, President Harry Truman had issued executive orders integrating the U.S. military and banning discrimination by the federal government. Over fierce objection from southern segregationists, Truman backed Hubert

Humphrey's call for a strong pro-civil-rights plank in the Democratic Party's national platform of that year.

Six years later, the Supreme Court issued the landmark ruling against racial segregation in schools in the *Brown v. Board of Education of Topeka* case. Accepting the arguments of Thurgood Marshall and the NAACP for the Brown family, the Court declared that "separate educational facilities are inherently unequal" and a violation of the Fourteenth Amendment. The *Brown* decision did not immediately end segregation in practice, and racial tensions grew substantially in the aftermath of the decision, stoked primarily by racist groups such as the White Citizens' Councils and the Ku Klux Klan, which fought integration through economic means and violent attacks on blacks. President Dwight Eisenhower was forced to call out federal troops to enforce the desegregation order in Little Rock, Arkansas as nine black students endured a mob-like mentality from whites in the community. The school eventually shut its doors for good to avoid integration. As President Clinton reflected in Little Rock on the fortieth anniversary of the desegregation of Central High, "What happened here changed the course of our country forever. Like Independence Hall where we first embraced the idea that God created us all equal. Like Gettysburg, where Americans fought and died over whether we would remain one nation, moving closer to the true meaning of equality. Like them, Little Rock is historic ground. For, surely it was here at Central High that we took another giant step closer to the idea of America."[11]

By the mid-1950s, it was clear to Martin Luther King Jr. and other emerging civil rights leaders that legal action alone was not sufficient to reverse the injustice of racial discrimination. Direct and sustained protest was needed to complement legal actions. With the advent of the civil rights movement, the United States entered perhaps its most transformative period of social reform and activism since the Progressive era. It came in powerful waves of action and reaction, culminating in the Civil Rights Act of 1964 and the Voting Rights Act of 1965.

The story of the civil rights movement is the story of leaders such as King, E. D. Nixon, Ralph Abernathy, Bayard Rustin, Fred Shuttlesworth, Fannie Lou Hamer, John Lewis, Julian Bond, Andrew Young, Jesse Jackson, James Lawson, James Farmer, Roy Wilkins, Whitney Young, and other leaders in the Southern Christian Leadership Conference (SCLC), the Student Non-violent Coordinating Committee (SNCC), the Urban League, the Congress of Racial Equality (CORE), and the NAACP. But it is also the story of thousands of less famous citizens who carried out the protests and the marches, participated in the sit-ins and Freedom Rides, supported the boycotts, endured the beatings and maltreatment of racist opponents, prayed for better days, and organized to create a nation that could finally live up to the stated ideals enshrined in Jefferson's founding creed and secured by Lincoln.

Although he proudly maintained that he served no ideological or partisan agenda, Martin Luther King Jr. should be considered a seminal figure in American progressive politics. King exemplified the progressive impulse to combine theory with action. He turned a personal philosophy focused on non-violence and humanitarian concern into concrete improvements for poor blacks and whites.

King's intellectual journey is informative and offers a nice map of how one builds a thoroughly progressive point of view on liberal social philosophy and religious ethics. He spent many years honing his personal framework through intense reading and writing on ancient philosophers, early Enlightenment figures, black intellectuals, and numerous theological figures. As Stephen Oates argues, King's eventual commitment to a theory of non-violent resistance emerged from his passion for the early Social Gospel teachings of Walter

Rauschenbusch combined with ideas about civil disobedience put forth by Henry David Thoreau and Mohandas K. Gandhi. This theory of non-violence was built on Thoreau's idea of "non-cooperation with evil" and love for one's enemies expressed through protests, marches, and boycotts combined with Gandhi's love for larger mankind and refusal to respond to hatred with hatred.[12]

Other King scholars, including David Chappell, note that his reading of Reinhold Niebuhr was equally important and provided him with a clear corrective to overly optimistic views about human nature in the Social Gospel and a more realistic stance about what he faced when confronting the evils of segregation: "Instead of assured progress in wisdom and decency, man faces the ever present possibility of swift relapse not merely to animalism but into such calculated cruelty as no other animal can practice. Niebuhr reminds us of this on every hand."[13]

Starting his career at the Dexter Avenue Baptist Church in Montgomery the same month that the *Brown* decision was handed down, King recognized that the South was at a turning point. Blacks either could continue to suffer grave injustices and violence at the hands of a white power structure that was only slowly being challenged, or they could take on the entire architecture of Jim Crow and finally force federal action through mass protest and civil disobedience.

E. D. Nixon, a former president of the Montgomery NAACP, agreed with King's sentiment and together with his NAACP colleague Rosa Parks and the Rev. Ralph Abernathy, helped to chart a new course of action for blacks starting with the Montgomery bus boycott. Parks famously refused to give up her seat on the bus to a white passenger, thus leading to her arrest for violating local segregation laws. This simple act sparked a firestorm of activity that would forever change the country. Although there had been previous bus boycotts in other cities, Parks's case provided a unique opportunity to build unified mass resistance to segregation among blacks while also providing a solid challenge to segregation laws at the federal level.

As the head of the newly created Montgomery Improvement Association, King overnight became the national leader of a new movement whose values and goals were powerfully expressed in his extemporaneous speech to launch the boycott:

> We're here in a general sense because first and foremost, we are American citizens, and we are determined to acquire our citizenship to the fullness of its meaning. We are here also because of our deep-seated belief that democracy transformed from thin paper to thick action is the greatest form of government on earth. . . . We are here this evening to say to those who have mistreated us so long that we are tired—tired of being segregated and humiliated; tired of being kicked about by the brutal feet of oppression. We have no alternative but to protest. . . . In our protest, there will be no cross burnings. No white person will be taken from his home by a hooded Negro mob and brutally murdered. . . . We will be guided by the highest principles of law and order. . . . If we protest courageously, and yet with dignity and Christian love, when the history books are written in the future, somebody will have to say, "There lived a race of people, of black people, of people who had the moral courage to stand up for their rights. And thereby they injected a new meaning into the veins of history and civilization."[14]

The black community successfully sustained the boycott for more than a year—despite violent mob attacks, bombings, and numerous legal proceedings—and in the process gained huge national attention to the cause of racial equality in the South. To illustrate the courage and strength of the regular citizens during the boycott, King would recount the story of an elderly woman who said (after King suggested that it would be okay for her to start riding buses again), "I'm gonna walk till it's over. . . . [M]y feet is tired, but my soul is rested."[15]

King, Parks, Nixon, and all of the other people who made the boycott successful decisively won their opening battle for equality when the Supreme Court in 1956 upheld a lower court ruling declaring the state and local bus laws unconstitutional. Building on the success of the Montgomery actions, two New York–based civil rights veterans, Bayard Rustin (who later organized the March on Washington) and Stanley Levison (a radical white attorney), helped King bring together other southern ministers to create the Southern Christian Leadership Conference—the organization that, despite ups and downs, would serve as the moral and political center of the civil rights movement for the next decade.

Joseph Lowery, one of the founding members of the SCLC, explained the critical role of the churches in the movement as resting on a belief by blacks that the "gospel was a liberating gospel, because when they read about God delivering Moses and the Children of Israel, they saw the parallel between the experience of the Israelites and the black experience . . . And so without always articulating it in theological terms, the black church has always seen God as identified with the downcast and the suffering."[16] The strong role of preachers in black communities helped to bring these teachings to life and spur moral activism. As David Chappell recounts, the movement thought of King as a divine leader—a modern-day Moses—who was leading a religious awakening as much as a political one.[17]

In addition to the black churches, students played a big role in the social activism and protest of the period. In early 1960, four freshmen at North Carolina A&T College in Greensboro, North Carolina, put their thoughts about injustice and non-violent resistance into action by calmly asking for coffee and doughnuts at a segregated lunch counter at a local Woolworth's. As recounted by Franklin McCain (one of the original members of the Greensboro sit-in), the four were denied service at the lunch counter despite having just purchased other goods in the store. The next day they returned with fifteen other students to occupy peacefully the seats at the counter; within two weeks, sit-ins were active in cities across the state.

As with the bus boycotts, sit-ins had been used for decades prior to 1960 by groups such as CORE and the NAACP. But the media exposure accorded the Greensboro sit-in galvanized students across the South—black and white—to stage their own challenges to segregation in various public settings. King invited the students to become the youth arm of the SCLC, but the students decided to start their own organization, the Student Non-violent Coordinating Committee. At first the students and the SCLC were deeply, if somewhat cautiously, in unison. Dr. King was famously arrested after a sit-in with students in Atlanta, and was greeted as a hero upon his return from Reidsville prison (after Robert Kennedy helped to orchestrate his release, thus starting the Kennedy brothers' slow but steady march to full support for civil rights). Over time, however, the two organizations would grow apart over substantial differences about the movement's goals, strategy, and views on "black power" in the mid-to-late 1960s.

In 1963, after an unsuccessful campaign against segregation in Albany, Georgia, the SCLC launched one of its most ambitious efforts in Birmingham, Alabama. Birmingham was one of the most segregated and repressive cities in the South and had a long history of violent oppression against union organizing and blacks. The city's public safety commissioner, Bull Connor, was a legendary segregationist whom the SCLC guessed it could goad into direct confrontation against non-violent resistors, thus exposing the dark underbelly of segregation in all its racist ignominy. The SCLC was correct in its estimation of Connor.

Beginning a targeted protest against the downtown commercial and municipal area, King and fourteen others were arrested by Connor's police force for violating a court injunction. While imprisoned, King wrote his famous "Letter from Birmingham Jail," a response to fellow ministers who had criticized King's course of action. Forcefully articulating the moral underpinnings of civil disobedience, King explained how his approach was the best way to achieve justice between two competing alternatives—the passive, wait-and-see complacency of the past and the more forceful and near-violent movement of the black nationalists represented by Elijah Muhammad and Malcolm X.[18] Just as progressives in the early days offered their path of social and economic reform as the solution to the extremes of laissez-faire and socialism, King positioned the non-violent civil rights movement as a distinctly American solution to injustice built on pragmatic action and Christian ethics.

Two weeks later, when Connor used dogs and fire hoses against peaceful teenage protestors, photos and television footage carried images of racist savagery around the world. After Connor's massive error, the tide turned heavily against the white establishment in the South as the brutality of segregation regularly appeared on television in homes across America and the globe. The SCLC eventually won an agreement with city leaders that met most of its demands in Birmingham: desegregation of stores, removal of segregation signs, lunchroom desegregation, expanded employment opportunities for blacks, and ongoing talks.[19]

Violence in Birmingham did not stop with a simple agreement, however. The temporary headquarters of the SCLC was bombed along with King's brother's house. Worse, a few months after the agreement the Ku Klux Klan bombed the spiritual home of the protests, the Sixteenth Street Baptist Church, killing four little girls.

The activism in Birmingham forever changed America's conception of racial relations and forced a sympathetic but somewhat passive Kennedy administration to back more aggressive federal civil rights legislation. In the summer of 1963, the movement hit new heights with the March on Washington and King's "I Have a Dream" speech. After JFK's assassination later that year, President Lyndon Johnson took up the cause of civil rights in earnest and, working closely with King and others, eventually turned Kennedy's presidential call for legislative action into the monumental Civil Rights Act of 1964—legislation that finally banned all discrimination based on race, religion, ethnicity, or sex in public accommodations, education, and employment. A follow-up bill passed in 1968 banned discrimination in housing.

One year later, after civil rights workers were killed in Mississippi and police clubbed and gassed marchers led by John Lewis and Hosea Williams in Selma, Alabama, the Voting Rights Act of 1965 was passed.* The Voting Rights Act banned literacy tests for voting, provided for the appointment of federal examiners to enforce the

---

*During the Carter administration I had the honor of working closely with John Lewis at the federal volunteer agency ACTION. A highlight of that relationship was when one particularly confrontational oversight hearing came to an abrupt end after a Republican committee member humiliated himself by demanding, voice steeped in outrage, why the federal government would even employ a "criminal" with a rap sheet as long as Lewis's was.

guarantees of the Fifteenth Amendment in districts with low percentages of registered minorities, and created Justice Department oversight of registration and voting laws. Even with these changes, progress was slow. In 1968, there were just twenty-nine black elected officials in Mississippi, a state with almost a million non-white residents. Towns that were 60 percent black had white mayors. There was just one African American mayor in the entire state, only one in the statehouse, and only one serving on a school board anywhere in the state. Things hadn't changed too much by 1972 when my brother and I first traveled to Mississippi. We were there not as election lawyers or poll watchers, but as campaign organizers recruited by civil rights champions like Charles Bannerman, who were then turning their attention to building the infrastructure needed to produce electoral success.

And things did start to change. Looking back, it is clear the combined effect of these laws and organizing was monumental in terms of opportunities for African Americans. The acts completely dismantled Jim Crow laws, which kept blacks from exercising their constitutional and human rights for more than a century. They opened the door for black participation in the political process and paved the way for the election of numerous black politicians at all levels of government. Measures of education, employment, income, wealth, and home ownership among African Americans all have risen dramatically in the aggregate since the passage of the acts. In fact, by the time I left the White House in 2000, Mississippi had more African American elected officials than any other state—almost nine hundred.

Unfortunately, as King recognized clearly before his murder, crushing poverty in the black community, and among white and Latino communities as well, would remain a major hurdle to advancement and equal rights for all. After Selma and the Voting Rights Act, King shifted his civil rights activism to focus on housing segregation in Chicago.

I remember television coverage of the Chicago Freedom Movement march through Chicago's white neighborhoods on the northwest and southwest sides, led by King, in 1966. In black and white, the images of enraged whites flinging curses and rocks at peaceful marchers were sickening. King—who himself was bloodied by a rock to the head—later said, "I have never seen so much hatred and hostility on the part of so many people."[20] It was a side of Chicago I had never seen. I attended integrated schools, and my parents—unusually, for their time—had black friends and coworkers with whom they socialized. Happily, Chicago is a much less divided city, but those horrific images taught me something about my city and myself, helped push me toward the progressive politics I was soon to embrace.

King created the Poor People's Campaign to fight for jobs, guaranteed income, and fair housing. About the same time, Cesar Chavez and the United Farm Workers extended the fight for economic justice through non-violent protests and strikes for higher wages and decent working standards for agricultural workers. Bobby Kennedy also brought issues of poverty and hunger to the forefront of American dialogue with his two-hundred-mile tour of Appalachia to assess the early results of the war on poverty, and later through his own presidential bid. Their work remains unfinished, and the search for jobs, housing, and solid education for millions of poor African Americans, Latinos, and whites remains a core civil rights challenge for progressives today.

The activism of the civil rights era also helped to galvanize the gay and lesbian community into heightened consciousness, stronger organization, and more aggressive stands for their own freedoms and rights. Gays and lesbians had toiled for decades for recognition and guaranteed legal rights before the politics of the late 1960s helped to sharpen their arguments and political efficacy. What began with resistance to a police raid of the Stonewall Inn in 1969 would eventually develop into the full-fledged GLBT civil rights movement in the 1980s that continues today.

I should note that the civil rights era not only represented the culmination of decades of struggle and action for progressives but also marked the starting point of the effective countermovement by conservatives to undo and reverse these gains. As President Johnson expected, the South was lost to the GOP and conservative forces after the passage of the Civil Rights and Voting Rights Acts. Barry Goldwater and Ronald Reagan, leaders of the burgeoning conservative counterinsurgency, campaigned ardently against the 1964 and 1965 acts as a violation of individual liberty and states' rights. Reagan later campaigned against fair housing legislation in his run for governor and delivered his first major address in the 1980 presidential race in Philadelphia, Mississippi, the city where the three civil rights activists were murdered in 1964.[21] Although conservatives would move away from their outwardly racist posture over time, the conservative movement gained its strength from the support of southern white voters and others opposed to racial equality.

We should recognize, as Senator Barack Obama candidly argued in his speech on race in Philadelphia, Pennsylvania, this year, that many working-class whites—who themselves never directly benefited from segregation or discrimination—feel resentment toward policies like affirmative action and busing that is grounded in legitimate concerns.[22]

But it is imperative that we have the courage to hold onto our principles in the face of lingering resentments and find ways to build common purpose across racial and class divisions. African Americans are not yet fully integrated into America's mainstream—the legacy of Jim Crow lives on in poor schools and blighted neighborhoods, in black unemployment and incarceration rates. We celebrate Senator Obama's historic achievement in being the first

African American to lead a major party ticket. But his achievement, which inspires all of us, does not mean our work is done. The challenges facing the African American community are challenges that affect everyone. And as we work to fight these ills, we also must try to build a multiracial coalition that can, in Senator Obama's words, "come together to solve a set of monumental problems—two wars, a terrorist threat, a falling economy, a chronic health-care crisis, and potentially devastating climate change; problems that are neither black or white or Latino or Asian, but rather problems that confront us all."

If the heroism of King and others during the civil rights movement teaches us anything, it is that we must fight and stand up for our beliefs no matter how hard our opponents might hit back. We must fight efforts to divide Americans along lines of race, gender, or sexual orientation, and instead find common ground and engage in a unified struggle to improve lives across all boundaries. It is incumbent upon all of us to make Martin Luther King Jr.'s dream of full economic and political equality a reality for all, rich and poor, black and white, gay and straight.

CHAPTER 4

LESSON FOUR

Progressives Stand for Universal Human Rights and Cooperative Global Security

Examining foreign policy from the 1900s through the Vietnam War, it is clear that the presidency of FDR (carried forward by his successor, Harry Truman) represented the high-water mark for progressivism in terms of establishing an intellectually and morally coherent approach to global affairs. All those who preceded or followed FDR added to the progressive vision in important ways, but ultimately they came up short in terms of articulating a set of principles and policies that the public understood and accepted for engaging the world and securing the nation. Although there were setbacks and missteps during his tenure, FDR's actions and ideas best capture the progressive moral commitment to human rights and the pragmatic desire to build an international architecture capable of advancing peace and prosperity.

FDR, aided by the circumstances of World War II, successfully integrated three key components of progressive thought into a viable security framework that both protected America and advanced its values: the just use of force, shrewd diplomacy, and the creation of international institutions to secure the peace; the development of a principled national purpose and a sense of shared sacrifice among the American public; and the political backbone and dexterity to fight our adversaries through both economic and military means.

This center spot in progressive national security thought took some time to develop. Early progressive reformers such as William Jennings Bryan and Robert La Follette were wary of getting involved in foreign affairs and warned about the perils of imperialism and war. Their opposition to foreign entanglements rested primarily on a continuation of the consensus isolationism and anti-imperialism that defined American foreign policy after the Civil War. Progressives such as La Follette also were concerned that mobilizing for war—specifically World War I—would undermine the larger cause of domestic reform, drain critical resources, and further entrench business in the machinations of government.

They correctly worried about the erosion of civil liberties, the propaganda and the strong-arming of dissidents that would accompany wartime efforts, and the potential vengeance associated with any victory. In this regard, history proved their fears well grounded. Wars have seemingly inevitably encouraged grievous violations of civil liberties, from the harassment of "hyphenated Americans" and the Palmer raids that arose out of World War I to FDR's internment of Japanese Americans during World War II, domestic spying during Vietnam, and today's suspension of habeas corpus, wiretapping program, satellite surveillance, and contempt for constitutional powers and international agreements condoning torture.

Other progressives, represented best by Jane Addams, were essentially pacifist in orientation. They believed in humanitarian internationalism but were ardently anti-war based primarily on their Christian ethics (although some pacifists were secular) and their beliefs about the counterproductive nature of military force in achieving American goals. A strong but typically small progressive pacifist strand has been present during nearly every major military conflict in the twentieth century, and in just about every case these progressives endured severe criticism from other Americans, and often fellow progressives, for their unwillingness to embrace war. This ridicule was particularly acute during World War I, when Addams was essentially disowned by pro-war progressives, and during World War II after the Japanese attacked Pearl Harbor.

The legacy of this wing of progressivism passed down through the years and was particularly prominent in response to Vietnam when New Left opposition to President Johnson and the "liberal" war in Southeast Asia echoed many of the same points argued by La Follette and Addams during World War I. Similar opposition developed among progressives in the lead-up to the Iraq War in 2003. Opposition to the Iraq War, however, was often more pragmatic and less isolationist than anti-war criticism in the past. Many progressive opponents of the Iraq War (including me) supported the U.S. invasion of Afghanistan as necessary and proper retaliation against the Taliban and al-Qaeda for its attacks on the United States on 9/11. They argued, correctly, that premeditated war in Iraq was strategically unsound, built on false assumptions, and diverted attention from the fight against global terrorists. Like La Follette and earlier progressives, they also argued that the war was part of a conservative effort to turn fear into political gain and exploit national grief and anxiety to advance a business-friendly economic agenda.

On the other side of the early progressive movement were outright imperialists such as Teddy Roosevelt and Herbert Croly, who argued vigorously for American strength abroad and actively tried to expand American possessions in other parts of the world. Leaders such as Woodrow Wilson and FDR put forth a far more productive and influential form of global engagement. The "liberal internationalist" position that began with Wilson and emerged solidly during World War II held that progressivism needed to "make the world

safe for democracy" through international law and order and cooperative military action when necessary.

As Michael Lind argues, these reformers stressed the practical
necessity of international engagement as a means to avoid turning
the U.S. into a permanent police state always on guard for attacks.[1]
At the same time, they extended the domestic banner of humanitarian concern for others to an international arena, arguing that human
dignity, positive liberty, and economic opportunity should be available to all. Many of these arguments were later incorporated into the
liberal anti-communism of Harry Truman and elite groups such as
Americans for Democratic Action during the Cold War. As Kevin
Mattson recounts, these committed internationalists later broke
apart over Vietnam—some became ardent supporters of the Vietnam
War (Johnson and his war cabinet) while others (like John Kenneth
Galbraith) viewed it as a serious mistake.[2]

The schism among progressives that began with World War I
had antecedents in the opposition to the conclusion of the Spanish-
American War and the U.S. takeover of the former Spanish territories of the Philippines, Cuba, Puerto Rico, and Guam that followed
in 1899. In response to America's new colonial aspirations, a cross
section of leading progressives and conservatives from Samuel
Gompers to Andrew Carnegie formed the Anti-Imperialist League
to fight the takeover of the Philippines and work to defeat future
policies of national expansion.[3] The league based its opposition to
imperialism on classic liberal grounds that it eroded liberty and national sovereignty and encouraged militarism. They branded the
occupation of the Philippines and the ongoing war against Filipino
nationalists to be "criminal aggression" (as opposed to William
McKinley's formulation of it as "benign assimilation") that violated
the principles of self-government enshrined in America's battle for
independence in 1776.[4]

Although the league lacked any real political power and would disband by 1921, the moral and economic ideas it expressed would find strong voices in American politics. Despite the conservative makeup of the league, it endorsed William Jennings Bryan in 1900 based on his strong anti-imperialist stand. Bryan, who initially supported the fight for Cuban independence during the Spanish-American War, became a powerful voice against American militarism and colonial aspirations in that election. As Michael Kazin recounts, Bryan's message against the Philippines war was not based on traditional isolationism but more on his Social Gospel principles "to respect the rights of others" and to "love thy neighbor as thyself." Bryan argued that McKinley's war of aggression would require permanent militarism and "turn the thoughts of our young men from the arts of peace to the science of war."[5]

Although a minority position, these ideas received extended treatment from progressives in the lead-up to and during World War I. Bryan again led the charge against imperialism as President Wilson's secretary of state. Bryan argued vigorously for the United States to remain neutral in the European conflict, and eventually resigned over the increasing discordance between his fight for peace and President Wilson's eventual desire to stop German military actions, particularly the use of submarine warfare. As Kazin explains, Bryan's chief argument was that America could not aid either side in war if it was to serve as an honest broker in what Bryan deemed an immoral conflict based on Europe's own imperialist desires. He also fought vigorously against "businessmen who sought to profit from the bloodshed"—a consistent refrain from progressives fighting the war.[6]

Similarly, Jane Addams founded the Woman's Peace Party to work against military conflict through mediation and to promote what Jean Bethke Elshtain labels the idea of "functional integration"—

increased social and economic ties between the nations of Europe and the United States to avoid war.[7] Addams and other progressives also strongly defended "radicals" and foreigners who were subjected to wartime harassment and repression by the Wilson administration and outside groups such as the American Protective League. Addams was denounced as a "Bolshevik" and a traitor for her efforts to defend civil liberties and political dissidents.[8]

As Eric Goldman recounts, Senators George Norris and Bob La Follette fought vigorously against U.S. entry into World War I in speeches that hit all of the progressive arguments at the time—the war was undemocratic; it would set back domestic reform; it would impinge on civil liberties; and it was designed to aid "the Morgans, the Rockefellers, the Schwabs, the Garys, the DuPonts and ... the thirty-eight corporations most benefited by war orders."[9]

Despite these fierce progressive protestations (many of which President Wilson shared until 1917), Wilson's later arguments against neutrality and in favor of intervention won the day among a much larger group of progressive activists and leaders. At the outbreak of war, an editorial in the *New Republic* announced the "end of American isolation," declaring that "the war has brought with it increasingly numerous and increasingly onerous American national and international obligations."[10] In supporting American participation in the war, progressives felt a sense of duty that necessitated an active role in world affairs to ensure that the peace was shaped fairly and in a manner consistent with U.S. interests.

Eventually acquiescing to these sentiments, Wilson laid out the principles for military intervention and a new internationalism in his war address to Congress on April 2, 1917:

A steadfast concert for peace can never be maintained except by a partnership of democratic nations. No autocratic

government could be trusted to keep faith within it or ob-
serve its covenants. It must be a league of honour, a partnership of opinion. . . . The world must be made safe for
democracy. Its peace must be planted upon the tested
foundations of political liberty. We have no selfish ends to
serve. We desire no conquest, no dominion. We seek no
indemnities for ourselves, no material compensation for
the sacrifices we shall freely make. We are but one of the
champions of the right of mankind. We shall be satisfied
when those rights have been made as secure as the faith
and the freedom of nations can make them. . . . It is a fearful thing to lead this great peaceful people into war, into
the most terrible and disastrous of all wars, civilization itself seeming to be in the balance. But the right is more precious than peace, and we shall fight for the things which we
have always carried nearest our hearts—for democracy, for
the right of those who submit to authority to have a voice
in their own governments, for the rights and liberties of
small nations, for a universal dominion of right by such a
concert of free peoples as shall bring peace and safety to all
nations and make the world itself at last free.[11]

It's instructive to note at this point that George Bush put forth
many of these same arguments in defending his decision to invade
Iraq in 2003. Bush essentially turned Wilson's visionary argument
for international engagement into cover for an extreme policy of
military aggression.

Progressives at the time rallied behind Wilson's bold experiment in applying domestic reform principles to the international
arena. The onset of war also provided an opportunity for economic

consolidation and reform on a much larger scale than had previously been attempted. As Harold Faulkner describes, the Wilson administration quickly moved to reconstruct American business and government along new lines to meet the demands of war, most prominently seen with the War Industries Board, which oversaw the "production of war materials along with the distribution of credit, fuel materials, and labor."[12] By most empirical standards, Wilson's war production effort was a genuine success and, as Arthur Schlesinger Jr. argues, it became the model for Franklin Roosevelt's later efforts to fight the Great Depression and win World War II.

After Word War I, Wilson wanted to avoid a punitive peace process that would do little to quell divisions in Europe or reduce the prospect of war. He outlined the basic structure of liberal internationalism and peacetime cooperation with his "Fourteen Points" speech to the Congress. Beyond a number of specific territorial issues in Europe, Wilson called for openness in diplomacy, increased free trade, freedom of the seas, reduction in arms, national sovereignty, and a "general association of nations" to maintain political solutions for international problems.[13] Unfortunately, the idealistic notions Wilson put forth would give way to severe steps to weaken the German military and force reparations for their war making at the Paris peace conference. The Treaty of Versailles forced Germany to accept sole responsibility for the war, give up territories to France and other nations, reduce its standing army, and pay serious reparations to the Allies, as Faulkner explains.

The treaty became the source of great progressive concern, prominently expressed by Herbert Croly in the New Republic, a strong supporter of the war. Croly argued that the sole purpose for engaging in the war effort was to commit "America to initiating and participating in the coming experiments in pacific international organization," which would demonstrate the country's willingness "to accomplish by other and more humane instruments the desirable objects which the world has hitherto accomplished by war."[14] Croly and other progressives believed the punitive nature of the treaty would create more wars within Europe rather than channeling conflicts into a peaceful resolution process that was promised in the new organization of nations. John Maynard Keynes's book on the Paris peace conference, *The Economic Consequences of the Peace*, solidified this position for many progressives by explaining how the harsh victory—primarily the undue reparations that would plunge Germany into further ruin—would undermine the larger cause of peaceful remediation.[15]

Wilson was able to salvage the League of Nations in the treaty, but that, in turn, served as the downfall to the treaty's passage in the U.S. Senate. Building on the ideas of international cooperation among nations, the League of Nations was designed to reduce armed conflict and settle differences between nations through a peaceful arbitration process where nations agreed to respect the sovereignty of one another and submit problems to a council of leading nations and a new court of international justice.[16] However, like the treaty itself, the League of Nations became a source of contention in American politics. Conservatives disliked it because of the implications for American sovereignty. Many progressives disliked it because it assumed that world powers would somehow put aside self-interest to pursue common goals. Many people on both sides simply opposed it to express their dissatisfaction with Wilson and his perceived poor handling of the war and its aftermath.

Although the ideas inherent in Wilsonian internationalism—support for global democracy, the creation of transnational institutions, and cooperation through international rules of law—would live and prosper in American foreign policy, the immediate effect of the failure of Versailles on progressivism was profound. The League of Nations, lacking the presence of the United States and any armed forces to back up its decisions, became an ineffective force for law and order and failed to prevent the rise of World War II. As historian Alan Brinkley details, mass arrests of labor organizers and leftist activists—described by President Wilson as hyphenated Americans who "have poured the poison of disloyalty into the very arteries of our national life"[17]—and the excesses of the Palmer raids soured the country on progressive nationalism and governance.[18]

Given these setbacks, progressive internationalist ideas would lie somewhat dormant until the rise of the totalitarian threat from Germany and Japan during World War II. Chastened by the experience of World War I, leading progressive intellectuals such as Charles Beard and John Dewey argued strenuously against intervention prior to 1941.[19] Conservative isolationism also reared its head in the form of the America First Committee (with its famous spokesman Charles Lindbergh), which was set up to fight for neutrality and oppose efforts by FDR to aid Britain and France through arms shipments and the passage of the Lend-Lease Act. But most of this opposition vanished with the Japanese bombing of Pearl Harbor as Americans of all stripes rallied to support the war effort and help the United States and its allies overcome the Axis powers. The declarations of war against Japan and Germany and Italy passed both the House and the Senate with just one dissenting vote.

The war effort itself constituted one of the most impressive national planning and coordination efforts in U.S. history. The level of shared sacrifice and common cause—from soldiers to civilians to businessmen to government officials—has never been matched in American life. As Harold Faulkner recounts, roughly sixteen million Americans went through military service during the war and nearly 95 percent of the nation's essential goods were rationed for civilians during the war.[20] Millions of Americans volunteered their services through homeland security efforts, medical assistance, war bonds, and programs to meet other critical domestic needs. Through a series of government agencies such as the War Planning Board and the Office of Price Administration, the Roosevelt administration shifted the entire engine of American manufacturing toward war needs, with American manufacturers eventually producing by 1944 approximately "187,000 planes, 68,000 tanks, 1,800,000 trucks, 2,800,000 medium and big guns, 15,000,000 machine guns and rifles, 43,000,000 rounds of ammunition, 43,400,000 bombs, 196,000,000 uniforms, and 98,000,000 pairs of shoes."[21]

The cause of progressive internationalism and the defense of democracy and human rights greatly expanded during World War II. Franklin Roosevelt articulated clear foundations for a just and peaceful world order with his stewardship of the Allied war effort. Building on the ideals expressed in his Four Freedoms address and the domestic agenda of the New Deal, President Roosevelt, along with British Conservative Party prime minister Winston Churchill, issued a joint declaration in 1941—called the Atlantic Charter—outlining a strongly progressive vision for postwar security and peace. The charter called for eight interrelated principles: no territorial gains for the United States or Britain, territorial sovereignty, the rights of all people to self-government, free trade, improved international labor standards and economic advancement, freedom from fear and want, freedom of the seas, and international agreements to end the use of force.

The Atlantic Charter was affirmed one year later in the Declaration by United Nations, and eventually served as the blueprint for the United Nations Charter in 1945. Replacing the failed League of Nations, the United Nations embodied the progressive desire for global cooperation grounded in mutual respect, peaceful conflict resolution (backed by peacekeeping forces of member nations), a belief in equal rights and self-determination for all people, and a commitment to humanitarianism. The UN Declaration of Human Rights was added in 1948 to commit the world's nations to the long-standing progressive principles that "[a]ll human beings are born free and equal in dignity and rights. They are endowed with reason and conscience and should act towards one another in a spirit of brotherhood."[22]

Although non-binding, the Declaration of Human Rights clearly established foundational rights for all people to political sovereignty and self-determination; fair legal protections; freedom of thought, conscience, action, and movement; the protection of family and property; and a host of economic and social basics including employment, equal pay, health care, food, housing, and education. Few documents have had more meaning to progressives. Eleanor Roosevelt, one of the document's drafters, proclaimed upon its signing, "This Universal Declaration of Human Rights may well become the international Magna Carta of all men everywhere . . . comparable to the proclamation of the Declaration of the Rights of Man by the French people in 1789, the adoption of the Bill of Rights by the people of the United States, and the adoption of comparable declarations at different times in other countries."[23]

Echoing the sentiments of Eleanor Roosevelt, President Jimmy Carter later made human rights the "soul of our foreign policy." As historian Douglas Brinkley recalls, Carter explained his position as consistent with America's deepest principles: "I like to try to make other people realize that our system works, that freedom of elections, freedom from persecution, that basic human rights being preserved, that a move towards peace, reduction in weapons, prohibition against suffering from inadequate health care and so forth are part of our national consciousness and that we can demonstrate that it works in this country and serves as an example to others."[24]

World War II was a great national triumph and a clear affirmation of progressive values built on national commitment to common purposes, the belief in essential human dignity and equal worth, and the necessity to fight for core democratic principles and establish new avenues for peaceful resolution of humanity's problems. The unity of spirit and commonality of purpose during the war exemplified progressives' belief in building a national and international community based on peace, human betterment, and individual advancement. That strain of progressive thought was later the core of President John F. Kennedy's eloquent, soaring inaugural address, and it found its direct manifestation in his founding of the Peace Corps, which to this day embodies that spirit.

However, the nature of World War II—a direct attack on U.S. shores and the brutality of Nazi Germany and imperial Japan— surely papered over significant differences in foreign policy thought that would soon emerge in the postwar era. The uncertainty about how to deal with the expanding Soviet empire and the potential for nuclear war following the U.S. use of the atomic bomb to end the war in the Pacific would create a number of divisions among progressives during the Cold War era. This fissure would become most pronounced with the rise of opposition to the Vietnam War.

The immediate challenge for progressives in the post–World War II period involved how best to challenge communism. President Truman adopted a strong stance against communist expansion, first with the Truman Doctrine, which offered economic aid and military support to Greece and Turkey in repelling Soviet ambitions, and shortly thereafter with the Marshall Plan, which provided $13 billion to help rebuild the economies of Europe and prevent the rise of communism in nations still in ruin from the war. As Arthur Schlesinger Jr. explained in *The Vital Center*, these twin efforts produced the core doctrine of liberal anti-communism: "One is the policy of *containment*: that is, the prevention of overt Communist aggression against states not now under Communist domination. The other is *reconstruction*:

that is, the removal in non-Communist states of the conditions of want and insecurity which invite the spread of Communism."[25]

Along with Truman's efforts at the presidential level, leading liberals such as Schlesinger, John Kenneth Galbraith, and Eleanor Roosevelt formed Americans for Democratic Action to help make the case for bringing together the cause of civil rights and economic freedom at home with firm anti-communism and American engagement abroad. Although consistent with earlier aims of Wilson and Roosevelt, this approach diverged from traditional progressive thought in important ways. As Kevin Mattson notes, the liberal anti-communism of ADA thinkers was built on a more pessimistic view of human nature that rejected ideas about man's essential goodness and progress that were explicit in Social Gospel teachings and pragmatic social thought at the turn of the century.

This line of thinking also firmly rejected the belief that there could be any acceptance of domestic communism within the larger liberal project. The ADA's posture of firmly rejecting "fellow travelers"—a term used by J. Edgar Hoover to designate people who were not themselves communists but who held sympathetic views to communism—was directly targeted at the perceived tolerance of communists within the 1948 Progressive Party (no relationship to earlier Progressive parties of TR and La Follette). Henry Wallace, former vice president to FDR and Progressive Party candidate for president in 1948, naively ignored this presence because he felt that "Red-baiting" and aggressive anti-communism directly threatened prospects for peace and international reconciliation. (Wallace himself was never a communist and opposed recognition of Soviet Russia earlier in his career, however.)

As Schlesinger and others argued, the political tolerance of an illiberal creed like communism, coupled with progressives' earlier isolationism, could not hold during a time of ideological struggle with a spreading Soviet empire. "Dough-faced" progressivism, in Schlesinger's formulation, needed to be replaced with firm anti-totalitarianism properly constrained by limited use of American military force when necessary.[26]

The practical application of many of these fiercely anti-communist positions quickly became problematic for many progressives, however. From the loyalty reviews ordered by President Truman to the overt Red-baiting of Joe McCarthy and Hoover, the fight against communism on the domestic front produced serious violations of civil liberties and freedom that echoed those from World War I and were ardently embraced by right-wing political groups. More important, this hard line of liberal thinking, taken to its extreme, contributed directly to the serious misjudgments and mistakes in Vietnam. Vowing never to bend to communist aggression anywhere in the world, President Johnson blindly escalated the war in Vietnam despite manifest failures in strategy and execution. As Kevin Mattson notes, strong liberal voices such as Galbraith and later Schlesinger opposed Vietnam, but their more subtle arguments about the need for military restraint were clearly lost in the fog of war.[27] The "liberal center" that emerged as a middle ground between pacifism and anti-imperialism on the far left and aggressive militarism on the far right quickly imploded through its own misapplication.

I entered presidential politics in 1968 at the height of the Vietnam War to try to move the country in a different direction at a time when the country was radicalized and the world was on fire. It was a natural step for a young person attending a college whose culture was rooted in its founding by abolitionists, which spawned the leading muckraking publication *McClure's,* which granted Abraham Lincoln his first honorary degree, and which hosted Lincoln and Stephen Douglas in the fifth of their famous clashes.

The war drew me into political activity, but for a while it was unclear whether I would find myself in a campaign headquarters or on the streets in protest. The two came together for me at the 1968 Chicago Democratic Convention. At that moment, it was unclear whether electoral change or direct action would be the more effective strategy for bringing peace—or if either strategy would work. But one thing was clear: those of us who were opposed to the war were right.

The war was a folly and a failure driven by dogmatic anticommunism that ignored the reality of the colonial origins of the war in Southeast Asia. It was never going to be "won" by sending in more troops or dropping more bombs. Regardless of what one thinks of their actions or culture, George McGovern and the protestors were correct to try to end the war. America would have been better off had Presidents Lyndon Johnson or Richard Nixon heeded their warnings earlier.

But anti-war actions had domestic political consequences as well. That McGovern was painted as weak and unfit to defend America has hung like a dark cloud over the progressive movement for more than thirty years, blocking the light that might have allowed us to see the disaster that the invasion of Iraq was destined to become.[28]

Progressives today need to put aside any lingering sentiment that Vietnam is an irremovable political albatross hanging around our necks. The notion—primarily concentrated among liberal hawks—that we need to act "tough" and suspend our empirical judgments on war because George McGovern got trounced in 1972 has led to tragic mistakes. Many Democratic leaders and Democratic national security experts who supported the Iraq resolution in the fall of 2002 and the invasion of Iraq in 2003 failed to carefully consider the consequences

of unilateral U.S. military action, failed to carefully read all of the intelligence estimates, and deeply misread post-9/11 politics and the lessons of the Vietnam War.

And like their liberal anti-communist counterparts during the
Cold War, too many contemporary liberal hawks joined right-wing
leaders in denouncing anti-war progressives as "soft" on terrorism.
Had these hawks been wise rather than dogmatic, they would have
recognized that, just as La Follette properly analyzed many of the
problems associated with World War I, the national security skep-
tics in the progressive movement correctly diagnosed the potential
perils of American militarism in Iraq.

The liberal hawks, at the end of the day, got not only the policy
wrong but the politics as well. Iraq has become for conservatives
what Vietnam was to progressives—a ball and chain dragging down
their credibility.

Looking back at all of this history, it is clear that progressives
during the Cold War—and now during the age of terrorism—have
had real difficulty in trying to find a sweet spot between their anti-
imperialist/isolationist strands and their internationalist/militaristic
ones. It is the unresolved tension between these intellectual traditions of progressivism—rather than the perceived excesses of either
tradition—that is primarily responsible for the incoherent public
presentation of their ideas today. As will be discussed in the final section, progressives can be ideologically firm in their opposition to radical Islamic threats and properly restrained in terms of when and how
best to use direct military action to fight this threat. This would bring
together both strands of progressive thought into a practical theory
that is internationally engaged and humanitarian in spirit yet realistic
and empirically grounded about American interests and how best to
fight those nations or groups that threaten our way of life.

PART TWO

From Clinton to Bush

Progressivism Versus Conservatism
A Millennial Clash

One hundred years ago, the question of the common welfare was at the heart of the policies adopted by Theodore and Franklin Roosevelt and others that produced the changes we now call the Progressive and New Deal eras. The first decade of the twentieth century was a time of uncertainty and extremism. The United States was undergoing a massive economic transformation from a primarily agricultural nation into an industrial economy. A concentrated group of corporations—ironically dubbed the "trusts"—ruled vast swaths of the new economy.

As we've seen, the challenge to the powerful elites of the Gilded Age came from the ranks of concerned activists, political movements, and muckrakers of various stripes. Their fights told the story of a nation that was abandoning its fundamental duty to protect its citizens. The dangers of leaving the public good in the hands of private interests struck Theodore Roosevelt as absurd: "Ruin in its worst form is inevitable," TR said, "if our national life brings us nothing better than swollen fortunes for the few and the triumph in both politics and business of a sordid and selfish materialism."

As president, Roosevelt moved to keep the special interests in check and helped to protect those who could not protect themselves. His government investigated monopolies, established the Department of Labor, passed the first laws to protect consumers from dangerous foods and drugs, and set aside hundreds of thousands of acres of our most beautiful lands to be shared by all Americans. The pattern of an activist government he set down outlasted his presidency.

In the first decade of the twenty-first century, the question of how best to define the common good still lies at the center of our political debate. The nation's transformation from an industrial economy to an information age economy has created enormous uncertainty and anxiety. Progressive achievements like Social Security and Medicare are under assault. A culture of "sordid and selfish materialism" flourishes as never before in a celebrity society. Our jungle is *Fast Food Nation* and our Standard Oil can be called Halliburton or Enron. Ken Lay was no Rockefeller, to be sure, but he is every bit as much the symbol of an era of corporate excess and manipulation as John D. was of unchallenged domination.

Forty years after they ventured into the post-Goldwater wilderness, radical conservatives successfully gained control of the White House, claimed the leadership of both houses of Congress, and have worked ceaselessly to re-create a nation in their ideological image. The elections of 2006 marked a clear break with this conservative ascendance and, I hope, the end of their reign. But the damage has already been done, and it will take many years and serious leadership to reverse the disastrous outcomes of Bush's presidency.

We now live in a country where almost everyone is working harder but where tax cuts go almost exclusively to the very wealthiest. We live in a nation where forty years of efforts to protect the natural environment now have been shredded like trees into wood chips. Where the oil companies write the energy policy. Where the pharmaceutical companies determine which of their products are safe. Where the line between lobbyists and legislators has disappeared. Where the lessons of creationism are taught alongside those of evolution while the health insurance system becomes more Darwinian every day. And all of this is presented to the American people live on Rupert Murdoch TV.

Who ushered in this conservative reign?

It was George W. Bush, the accidental president and standard-bearer of modern conservatism, who has cheerfully cast aside his family's sense of noblesse oblige with a self-imposed mission to oblige the nobility. He lives and breathes in a shame-free zone where killing the death tax is priority one, the bodies of returning soldiers from Iraq are blocked from view, and Saddam Hussein was complicit in the attacks of 9/11.

This is dramatically different from the time I spent in the Clinton administration. Say what you will about my former boss (and there is no shortage of opinions about the man), in manner, beliefs, governing philosophy, and legislative actions President Clinton was—and is today—a deeply progressive figure. To me, Clinton represents the practical progressivism backed by core moral principles that marked the early progressive reformers. Grounded in his family history, a rich faith, and concern for others, President Clinton embodied the progressive legacy of policy experimentation to ensure that government worked for people and focused on national needs. His primary mission as president was to manage a rapidly changing economy and security environment to the benefit of people here and abroad.

The focus of the next two chapters will be on how the wildly divergent presidencies of these two men—William J. Clinton and George W. Bush—represent the opportunities and limitations of progressive governing versus the manifest failure of conservatism in practice.

CHAPTER 5

Bill Clinton

A Modern Progressive

Many of us who got our first taste of politics in Eugene McCarthy's 1968 anti-war presidential campaign went to Connecticut for the 1970 Senate campaign of the Rev. Joe Duffey, where I first met Bill Clinton. Duffey, the son of a coal miner, had worked his way through college and had become an ethics professor at a local seminary and a leader in Connecticut's anti–Vietnam War movement. My older brother, Tony, signed on as Duffey's campaign manager, and I followed, as did Bill Clinton and a number of other young activists.

The incumbent, conservative Democrat and Vietnam hawk Tom Dodd (Senator Chris Dodd's father) decided early on not to run for reelection. He was in poor health and had been censured by the U.S. Senate for alleged misuse of campaign funds. In those days, the Connecticut Democratic Party chose its Senate candidates at a statewide nominating convention, which meant that in most years the party bosses could name the candidate of their choice without the voters having a say.

In 1970, party regulars wanted to replace Dodd with an attorney named Al Donahue; Duffey was considered too liberal to carry a state that had been sharply divided, as the nation had been, by the war. But Duffey picked up enough delegates at the convention to finish second and to force a primary, which he won. Senator Dodd then reentered the race, running as the de facto conservative alternative to Duffey and to Lowell Weicker, a liberal Republican who, in an odd historical twist, later lost his senate seat to Joe Lieberman, left the Republican Party, and was elected governor of Connecticut as an independent, only to see Lieberman leave the Democratic Party to be reelected as an independent. Connecticut can be a strange place.

It was a tough race. Connecticut should have been a Democratic state, but Duffey was an outsider and Weicker was able to run as the moderate alternative to Duffey and to the more conservative Dodd—kind of a "third way" candidate more than twenty years before the term was applied to Bill Clinton and the United Kingdom's Tony Blair. Bill Clinton showed his gifts early on. I'm not going to pretend that I looked across the room after a late-night strategy session and said to myself, *"That guy is going to be president someday,"* but he was smart as hell and a tireless worker, and he had a gift for getting to the heart of whatever issue was on the table, whether it was canvassing strategy or tax policy.

In the end, Weicker won by 90,000 votes, with Dodd taking more than 260,000 "Democratic" votes from us. For campaign workers such as Bill Clinton, my brother, and myself—young people just a few years away from our own blue-collar upbringings—it was discouraging to see a coal miner's son beaten in large part because we couldn't hold the gritty working-class cities and towns that were the backbone of Connecticut's Democratic vote. I don't know if we ever could have overcome the divide opened up by the Vietnam War to win that race. But I do know that we never forgot what happens to progressive candidates when they can't connect with families that live on hourly wages and see foreign policy as an essential part of the patriotism they proudly wear on their sleeves.

Bill Clinton and I got to work together again two years later in the McGovern presidential campaign. Clinton ran the Texas campaign with Taylor Branch. It was the beginning of the end of our ability to hang on to white working-class voters in presidential races in the South, a crucial lesson that was not lost on Clinton in his later campaigns for attorney general and governor in Arkansas.

After the McGovern campaign, I went off to law school, graduating from Georgetown in 1976, and then worked a series of Washington jobs, first as a trial attorney in the Justice Department, then as a political appointee of the Carter administration at the ACTION agency, and then as a staff counsel on Capitol Hill. It was illuminating to see the way Washington worked under Reagan and the Republican Senate majority that swept in with him in the 1980 election.

Ronald Reagan was in large part the product of a fifteen-year effort by conservative elites to roll back the progressive gains that began with the New Deal, and to retake political and economic power. It wasn't exactly a "vast right-wing conspiracy," but it was a well-funded network of think tanks, activists, pundits, and elected officials who were determined to move the country to the right and made no secret of their disdain for progressive ideals.

From the moment Ronald Reagan announced his campaign to his last day in office, it was clear that Reagan wasn't just fighting the Democrats but trying to roll back eighty years of progressive policies in a way that Nixon and Eisenhower had never attempted. His economic vision centered on tax reductions for rich Americans. He specialized in union busting (including the firing of eleven thousand striking air traffic controllers) and the gutting of agencies that protected Americans' environment, health, and safety. The Iran-contra scandal made clear the Reagan administration's contempt for the law and the Constitution.

Today, America has entered an era of great nostalgia for Ronald

Reagan because of his unbridled optimism and relationship with Mikhail Gorbachev. But I remember Ronald Reagan differently. He was the president who did nothing as middle-class wages eroded and corporate profits and senior executives' salaries soared. He was the president who engineered the transformation of our natural resources from public treasure to private spoils. He was the chief executive who said nothing for seven years as thirty-six thousand AIDS cases were reported in the United States and twenty-one thousand Americans died (many more, by some estimates) because, as his surgeon general, C. Everett Koop, explained it, "the president's advisers took the stand, 'They are only getting what they justly deserve.'"[1] Reagan helped convert religion from unifying force to divisive dogma, building a bridge from the racism of Nixon's "southern strategy" to the homophobia of Bush's 2004 campaign and the xenophobia to which Republicans have hitched their wagon today. Yes, President Reagan's government did include some notable and important public servants: James Baker at Treasury, George Shultz at State, and White House chief of staff Howard Baker. But his administration also had Jim Watt, Anne Gorsuch, Sam Pierce, Ollie North, and John Poindexter—whose extremism, incompetence, and corruption made them poor public servants.

Conservatism has its strengths—its love of country, its appreciation of faith, and its skepticism of what government should do (a healthy skepticism that should be applied to every large institution). But the conservatives in power during the Reagan years were as bad as we'd always thought—they represented the dark side of the American character, a selfishness and intolerance at odds with everything I believed in and what I know America has stood for.

I supported Clinton's candidacy not only because we were twenty-year veterans of the same political wars but also because I felt he had a strong grasp of the challenges America faced at a time of change. The Republican Party was trying to drag America back to an age that never really existed. At the same time, many Democrats were trying to apply old solutions to a new set of problems, holding tight to inflexible orthodoxies—no matter if they still held true or not. Clinton understood that it was the principles behind his progressive vision that were sacred, not particular policies or regulations, and that the first priority of our federal government must be that every American share in the great gifts America could bestow.

His campaign theme summed it up perfectly: "Putting people first."

I also liked the fact that, as complicated a man as Bill Clinton is—and as nuanced as his understanding of history, economics, and politics could be—he was brilliant at getting straight to the point. That's why the sign James Carville hung in the Little Rock headquarters was such an apt reflection of Clinton's approach: "Change vs. more of the same; the economy, stupid; don't forget health care." Clinton recognized that the world had changed, and his first priority was clearing a path for success for the broad middle class and those striving to climb into it. These were the people who'd cost McGovern and Duffey their elections; these were the folks at the heart of the progressive movement's concerns. And they weren't abstractions to me. These voters were my parents, my cousins, my aunts, and the other people I grew up with. They were people like me.

Although my role in the campaign wasn't of war-room legend, I helped Clinton prepare for the debates with President Bush, and when it was offered, I jumped at the opportunity to work in the White House. I saw in the Clinton administration a chance to get America back on course, and I was eager to help in any way I could. So in January 1993, I found myself leaving the company I had started with my brother and joining the White House, as staff secretary to President Bill Clinton.

I've never forgotten the day Bill Clinton was sworn in. I attended the inaugural ceremony at noon and met briefly with the president on official business in the President's Room at the Capitol immediately after. By one o'clock I was back at the White House, entering the gate while tourists strained to see if I was someone "important." I stopped for a moment to watch the old drapes coming down in the Oval Office and the new official portraits going up. It was an emotional moment for the son of a man who ran a cutting machine in a factory for fifty years: witnessing, and being a small part of, the peaceful transition to a new administration in the most powerful nation on earth.

In his memoir, President Clinton writes that the stream of history is in large part "the story of our efforts to honor our founders' charge 'to form a more perfect union,'" and that "when change is forced upon us by events, we are all ... thrown back on our fundamental mission to widen the circle of opportunity, deepen the meaning of freedom, and strengthen the bonds of community."[2]

The world had changed dramatically since a Democrat had occupied the Oval Office—the Soviet Union had fallen, electronic communications and global trade were exploding, and middle-class support structures from schools to health insurance to workplace protections were fraying—and conservatism was taking us in the wrong direction.

We were sailing into uncharted waters. We did have a compass we could rely on: the progressive values that had guided America to greatness and prosperity. As President Clinton would tell the nation a few weeks after his inauguration: "I believe we will find our new direction in the basic old values that brought us here over the last two centuries: a commitment to opportunity, to individual responsibility, to community, to work, to family, and to faith."

But we were facing a determined opposition led by Newt Gingrich, who wanted to chart a very different path for America.

Much has been made and written about the administration's rough start—the nominations that blew up and the mistakes of a rookie White House staff. Despite the start-up hassles, let the record show that President Clinton hit the ground running. Even before he'd addressed Congress and the nation, just twenty-seven days into his presidency, he'd signed the Family and Medical Leave Act into law, sending a clear, strong message: even in a competitive world, we can find a way for mothers to tend to sick children, or for daughters and sons to spend time with their dying parents. Profit is important, but family is, too. It was truly putting people first.

Just days after the Family and Medical Leave Act was signed, the president addressed a joint session of Congress for the very first time.

While acknowledging "that the real engine of economic growth in this country is the private sector, and . . . each of us must be an engine of growth and change," President Clinton told the nation: "Tonight I want to talk with you about what government can do because I believe government must do more." He positioned government as a force for positive change, and explained that government really could work for the American people if it understood the challenges they faced and the progressive values that made America strong.

That was just the beginning. The first two years of the Clinton administration were extraordinarily productive. Yes, the president's health care reform package came to a brutal and untimely end. But, contrasted with four years of drift during Reagan's second term and four years of gridlock under George H. W. Bush, the president's achievements were truly remarkable.

The president's first focus was the economy. It's a cliché to say that the best social program is a job, and talk about putting the American Dream within reach of every working American has long been a soapbox staple. It doesn't make those ideas any less true or any less important. And that's what made Clinton's first budget central to his presidency.

By 1993, years of huge federal deficits had sapped confidence in America and forced interest rates up for everybody. The federal government was bidding against businesses and homeowners for billions of dollars in foreign capital every month. This not only gave investors in Japan and Western Europe (China was only just emerging as the economic giant it is today) more control over our economy than we wanted. It made it more expensive for businesses large and small to invest and for regular Americans to achieve the security that comes with homeownership or a college education.

If the deficit came down, interest rates would follow; with the costs of investment and innovation reduced, we believed, the American economy would blossom. But we weren't willing to balance the budget on the backs of middle-class Americans, who were already weighed down by a sluggish economy and declining government services. Clinton believed that the burden of deficit reduction should largely be borne by the people who had benefited most from the Reagan tax reductions twelve years earlier: large corporations and America's most affluent earners. (And, of course, the tax increase turned out to be an excellent investment for them, as profits and the return on private investment soared in the Clinton economy.)

And even though we knew there had to be budget cutbacks, we weren't going to ignore the needs of working families; Bill Clinton had said many times on the stump, "No one with children who works full time should live in poverty." So we found money to double the Earned Income Tax Credit, a refundable tax credit that goes to low-income working families with children. We strengthened the Community Reinvestment Act, which directs banks to invest in businesses and in-dividuals in economically depressed communities. We put funds into infrastructure projects that could help strengthen the overall economy and create good blue-collar jobs. We kept education funding high, so that every child would have a chance to succeed. And we created a new way for young people to work in troubled communities, enhancing public health, education, the environment, and their own understand-ing of the challenges our nation still faces.

We believed that young people of that era had the same desire to give back to their nation and to help fellow Americans in difficult circumstances that pushed so many members of my generation into political activism and organizations like the Peace Corps. And so we found money to create AmeriCorps, a service organization that put highly motivated young people into some of America's most disad-vantaged communities: teaching and mentoring children, helping to build affordable housing, cleaning parks and open spaces, and build-ing the capacities of communities to organize themselves. Since 1993, more than two hundred thousand Americans have served in AmeriCorps—more than have served in the Peace Corps' entire forty-seven-year history.

Not a single Republican in either house voted for the budget—a budget that paved the way for an economic boom that, for the first time in twenty years, lifted the economic status of the middle class. The bond markets got the lion's share of the credit for recognizing that our commitment to deficit reduction was real and for letting interest rates drift down. But that was only part of the story. Our budget put America on the path to prosperity because it truly in-vested in America and its people.

The president signed other proposals into law that strengthened families and helped make life better for all Americans—but especially middle-class Americans and the working poor—and expended immense political capital to get them. We passed the Brady Bill, which kept more than half a million felons, fugitives, and domestic abusers from buying guns. We put a hundred thousand new police officers on the street, which ultimately contributed to the sharpest drop in crime the United States had ever known. And we banned assault weapons, whose only purpose was to help criminals kill people with horrifying speed.

These were important achievements, but it was the economic plan that produced truly spectacular results. When Bill Clinton was sworn in, the unemployment rate was over 7 percent and hadn't been below 5 percent for twenty years. Eighteen months into the Clinton administration, the unemployment rate dropped below the 6 percent mark, and by the time Clinton left office, the unemployment rate had been below 5 percent for forty-four consecutive months.[3] For African Americans and Hispanics, groups for whom the American economy had never worked well, the unemployment rate fell to levels not seen in decades.[4]

And our eight years in office saw the full flowering of America's information economy—a transformation that has touched almost every aspect of our lives and clearly showed American technological and economic leadership. Support for science and technology—both pure research and practical applications—in combination with low interest rates and high demand meant that technology firms from Silicon Valley to Silicon Alley (the name given to New York City's high-tech community in Lower Manhattan) had the support and customers they needed to expand, create jobs, and generate profits. President Clinton and Vice President Gore "got" technology, and their efforts to get it into government agencies and inner-city schools helped ensure that everyone benefited from the technology revolution and was able to contribute to its next wave.

I'm extraordinarily proud of what the Clinton administration did for working families. Nonetheless, the failure of the Congress to approve health care reform still stings.

Hillary Clinton did an extraordinary job mastering the complicated details of America's health care system and crafting a plan that would have had profound benefits for millions of Americans—bold and necessary reform. But if the Republican decision to block health care changes for political advantage hurt in those days, it is felt even more painfully today, especially by the middle class.

To Mrs. Clinton's credit—and that of many others in the administration—we continued to work on important health care reforms despite our setbacks, and notched important successes over the next six years. We created the State Children's Health Insurance Program, which today covers more than six million kids, most in working families.[5] And we changed the law to make health insurance portable, so that if you changed jobs you didn't immediately lose your care. And we passed a law so that people with disabilities could keep federal coverage if they went to work. By the time Bill Clinton left office, the percentage of insured Americans was climbing.[6] Since 2000, however, the situation has changed dramatically. The number of uninsured Americans has risen almost 20 percent since 2001, to forty-seven million.[7] In President Clinton's last year in office, the average annual cost of health insurance for a working family was about $6,100.[8] Now it costs twice as much, more than $12,100 a year—a staggering increase that affects virtually every aspect of the economy.[9]

Today, factory workers and owners are competing against foreign manufacturers, whose health care costs are covered by national insurance, giving them a tremendous cost advantage over American producers. Many small-business owners can't afford to insure their employees at all, while millions of employees work full-time without insurance. Even workers who have insurance have seen annual out-of-pocket premium contributions double, to $3,200.[10] The result: thousands of people who get sicker than they need to get or die before they should, while we all share the expense of the uncompensated care doctors and hospitals provide for the uninsured.

We wanted badly to change all of that. Universal health care has long been a staple of affluent democracies around the world. President Johnson made a gigantic down payment with Medicare and Medicaid for older Americans, the poor, and the disabled. Presidents Roosevelt, Truman, Eisenhower, and Nixon had tried to reform the system and failed. We thought we could finish the job.

Of course, we made our share of mistakes. A task force that operated in secret assembled the plan, a plan whose features were so tightly linked that the perfect became the enemy of the good—no one part of the plan could be tweaked for practical or political reasons without the whole of it collapsing.

But there was a lot to recommend in our plan as well. The Clinton strategy dodged the trap that earlier attempts at reform had fallen into—it avoided calls for a single-payer system, which would have disrupted people's existing coverage—while preserving the goal of excellent, universal care. Under the plan, everybody contributed: most Americans would have continued to get their insurance through work. Small businesses would have been given access to discounted plans, underwritten by a cigarette tax. Insurers would have been restricted in their ability to cherry pick patients, ensuring that even individuals with preexisting conditions could get coverage and care. Pharmaceutical companies would negotiate prices, rather than imposing them, as part of a major effort to slow health care cost inflation.

Unfortunately, enough special interest groups saw a threat to their profits that they launched a multimillion-dollar ad campaign against it. Leading conservative strategists pressured Republican senators to kill the bill with a filibuster, allowing a minority of the Senate to smother health care reform—not because health care didn't need reform, but because Republicans didn't want to give the Democrats a key political victory in an election year.

Health care reform never made it to a floor vote. Today, we remain the only affluent democracy in the world where you can hold down a full-time job and still not be able to afford a trip to the doctor.

In the fall of 1994, with the failure of health care reform looming over us, the Republicans won control of both the U.S. Senate and the House of Representatives. The era of investigations and personal attacks on the Clintons were upon us. What started as a struggle for political power ended in a bitter personal war between the Gingrich-DeLay Congress and the Clinton administration. Some thought the administration would essentially be over by 1995—a demise famously and prematurely announced by Republican senator Phil Gramm after his party's 1994 triumphs.

Fortunately, Clinton's political decline was exaggerated. During his second campaign, Clinton spoke often of his eagerness to build a "bridge to the twenty-first century." But even in the darkest moments of 1995 and 1996, the president was laying the foundations for a bridge meant to "help our parents raise their children, to help young people and adults to get the education and training they need, to make our streets safer, to help Americans succeed at home and at work, to break the cycle of poverty and dependence, to protect our environment for generations to come, and to maintain our world leadership for peace and freedom."

Clinton's bridge was built on a progressive foundation. And one critical support beam of the structure was a new way of dealing with globalization, whose extent and effect on American workers we were just beginning to grasp. We understood that in an age of instant global communications and emerging economies, we had to engage in the global economy, but not by surrendering to what Ross Perot had called an economic "race to the bottom," where we competed by easing environmental regulations and allowing wages to fall to developing-world levels.

Rather than bringing America down, it was important that the global economy lift up other nations and make life better for them and for us, through cheaper goods for American consumers and new markets for our own products and services.

We also understood that we couldn't weigh the benefits of trade merely by looking at the aggregate effects on GDP. Even then, it was becoming apparent that the benefits and the drawbacks of trade were being unevenly distributed. The system was more concerned with the free flow of capital and stable marketplaces, while workers' rights and environmental protection were overlooked.

President Clinton recognized this early on during the debate over the North American Free Trade Agreement (NAFTA), which President George H. W. Bush had signed. Clinton pledged that he would negotiate side agreements on labor rights and environmental protections so that increased trade would lift wages south of the border, not lower them in the United States, and that incentives for any of the three North American nations to gain competitive advantage by cutting environmental corners would be removed. He achieved these goals and, ultimately, strong hemispheric economic growth.

Of course, NAFTA isn't perfect. The intersection of open trade policies and U.S. agricultural subsidies has combined to force some of the poorest Mexican farmers off their land. It became clear that labor and environmental standards cannot be left to side agreements and need to be part of a core agreement, with violators subject to sanctions—as Clinton himself argued near the end of his administration. That is why NAFTA has spurred a healthy debate in 2008 about whether the agreement needs to be reviewed and modernized.

I hope that the debate goes forward. But I also hope it reflects two important developments. First, the United States created twenty-three million jobs during the Clinton administration while middle-class incomes grew faster than at any time in three decades, all with NAFTA in effect. Second, it is the rapid industrialization of China and the breathtaking growth in India, not Mexico, that are the sources of unprecedented change and challenges in the global economy today.

We also worked hard to open foreign markets to our goods and saved consumers around the globe $740 billion a year when tariff barriers fell.[11] We helped establish the World Trade Organization, giving the United States a forum in which to protest unfair trade that hurt American workers. At the same time, we tried to provide for the workers who might be displaced by globalization both by beefing up our export promotion activities and by increasing funding for training of displaced workers. It was critical to us that trade benefit Americans at every income level.

Trade barriers weren't the only things in the way of American workers. In a global economy, American industries couldn't compete on the basis of cheap labor, and so the president committed to increasing aid to America's schools. He reformed the college loan system to make it easier, simpler, and less expensive, and he significantly expanded the work-study and Pell Grant programs. By the end of the administration, ten million families were using the new HOPE Scholarships and Lifetime Learning tax credits to help pay for college.[12]

Fundamental to President Clinton's philosophy was the importance of work to an individual's sense of self and well-being. He approached welfare reform not as a punitive act, meant to punish the lazy and irresponsible, but as a way of creating opportunity for those who had few options in their lives. He showed this philosophy in the vetoes of Republican budgets that shut down various parts of the federal government during the winter of 1995–96, when the partisan majority tried to reform welfare without the training, day care, transportation assistance, and counseling provisions needed to ensure that poor people were being prepared for success and not kicked aside. President Clinton's idea was to extend a hand up—to help people like those he'd grown up with build the skills and values needed to move up America's economic ladder. He often talked about a young boy he'd met who told him that the best thing about welfare reform was that "when someone asked him what his mother did for a living," the child now had an answer.

My father held two jobs in his life, twenty-five years each. He took the first job in 1925, cutting cardboard in a Chicago factory, for one of the few companies that did well enough to keep workers on the line continuously during the Great Depression. He used to tell a story—over and over again, the way fathers will when they're trying to teach you a lesson—about a man who came to work as my father's assistant on the line. It was maybe 1934, and the worst had passed, but good times were a long way off. The man punched in, walked over to meet my father, and began sobbing. And when my father asked him why, he found that it was because the man hadn't worked in two years. He hadn't had a way to feed his family, hadn't been able to look at himself in the mirror, really. So that first hour on the job was the most important and wonderful thing that had happened in his life for twenty-four long months.

It's a lesson that stuck with me. Jobs are more than just a paycheck—they're important in ways that people who haven't spent time out of work sometimes do not understand.

As important as the Clinton administration's policies were in bringing down the cost of capital and increasing investor confidence, steps to prepare people for jobs in the new economy were just as important. Not everybody can be a scientist or an engineer. But all of us can come home from a hard day's work proud of what we've done. Our spending as consumers helped fuel the technology boom, too. And after years of economic malaise, we saw jobs created in communities across America at every level, proving once again that we were still the world's most dynamic economy.

The Clinton years also saw a dramatic change in the global security system. With the collapse of the Soviet Union, the United States military was able to refocus its mission. In 1993, we learned where that focus needed to be when a car bomb exploded below the North Tower of the World Trade Center. Not nearly the magnitude of the September 11 attacks, this attack (which killed six and injured over a thousand), and the bombing of the Alfred P. Murrah Federal Building in Oklahoma City two years later, made clear the threat to our homeland posed by foreign and domestic terrorists.

President Clinton acted aggressively to shift priorities not only in the military but also in the intelligence agencies that would be of primary importance in monitoring terrorists' actions within the United States and abroad. Yet we were still learning the limits of conventional power when faced with unconventional enemies. In 1996, terrorists blew up a truck bomb just outside Khobar Towers, near Dhahran, Saudi Arabia, killing nineteen U.S. airmen and one Saudi national. In 1998, 257 people, including 12 Americans, were killed when terrorists linked to Osama bin Laden's network blew up car bombs at the American embassies in Tanzania and Kenya. In the aftermath of these attacks—and after working with local officials to disrupt another planned embassy bombing, this one in Tirana, Albania—the United States attempted to kill bin Laden at a meeting in Afghanistan. Unfortunately, bin Laden left the targeted area a few hours before the missile strike, and survived to kill again.

We achieved some success. In 1995, we worked with local authorities to stop a plot to blow up a dozen planes flying from the

Philippines to the West Coast of the United States. A conspiracy to blow up the Holland and Lincoln Tunnels in New York was uncovered in 1999. And as the turn of the millennium approached later that year, we broke up a series of plots designed to turn that evening of celebration into a night of tragedy. Around the world, we were able to celebrate the new millennium in peace and security.

While we were shifting the focus of our special forces, law enforcement, and intelligence agencies, we were learning to deploy our traditional military and diplomatic assets abroad in ways that projected America's progressive values into some of the world's most troubled regions. We helped broker a lasting peace in Northern Ireland, ensuring civil rights for the region's Catholic minority. We used military power and negotiating pressure to bring peace to Bosnia and nurture democracy there after a bloody civil war killed a hundred thousand people and displaced a million more. And in Kosovo, beginning in 1998, another U.S.-led NATO intervention brought to an end another bloody conflict and demonstrated to Muslims around the world that our commitment to justice and peace knows no ethnic boundaries. We had other peacemaking and peacekeeping successes in forgotten corners of the world from East Timor to South America, and one spectacular failure that haunts us all to this day—the failure to intervene rapidly in the Rwandan genocide.

If the concept of global warming was almost unknown by the American public at the beginning of the Clinton administration, it was a national priority by its close. The administration's commitment to greenhouse gas reduction found its expression in the president's embrace of the Kyoto accords and the global leadership on the issue by Vice President Al Gore.

My position as White House chief of staff gave me the opportunity to help lead one of the administration's other key environmental initiatives: preserving America's wilderness. Not since Teddy

Roosevelt has any president protected so much of America's dwindling open spaces. Under President Clinton, the National Park System expanded by more than four million acres, as thirteen new national park areas were created and others—including Joshua Tree and Death Valley National Parks—were significantly expanded. Working with Secretary Bruce Babbit at the Department of the Interior, Secretary Dan Glickman at the Department of Agriculture, and the Environmental Protection Agency administrator Carol Browner, we designated seventeen new national monuments, protecting everything from groves of California redwoods to Abraham Lincoln's summer home in Washington, D.C. And tens of millions of acres of national forest were protected from exploitation and development. Even though the Bush administration has done its best to undo regulations that would have permanently protected an additional sixty million acres of roadless forest from road building and timber harvests, President Clinton's environmental legacy will be enjoyed by millions of Americans for generations to come.

That being said, in some ways we missed the magnitude of some of the changes taking place in the world around us. There was a tendency to look backward—to see the problems that had been with us for many years, ignored or exacerbated by conservative policies of twelve years of Reagan and Bush—rather than look ahead. Just as it is easier now to look back and suggest that we should have acted more boldly to address terrorism than it is to know what new challenges are emerging ahead of us, it was easier then to identify the budget deficit and welfare reform as challenges than to predict the coming dislocations in the global economy.

In addition, the world clearly moves faster today. If we underestimated the full effects of globalization, it is at least in part because nations such as China and India spent almost forty years as economic basket cases—and then emerged as global competitors in little more than a decade. The pace of global warming is accelerating as populations, economies, and the greenhouse gasses they produce grow at a geometric clip. Political movements and terrorist organizations use the Internet to grow from local insurgency to global threat within a few short years. Trapped in the slow-motion worlds of Washington, D.C., and global policy making, we were not as quick as we should have been to pick up on some important developments.

Of course, there was also the six-year slow drip that was Whitewater, a partisan inquisition run by a prosecutor with a deep ideological animus against what the president was trying to accomplish. And it carried other costs. Our attempt to kill Osama bin Laden in Afghanistan in August 1998 and the missile attacks on Baghdad in December 1998—which occurred after Saddam Hussein forced UN weapons inspectors out of Iraq—were denounced by Republicans as wag-the-dog diversions. Serious Republicans in the Congress defended the president's actions in the interests of our national security. But there were many in power far more interested in partisan attacks.

This was fueled by personal mistakes made by the president and by the poisonous partisan atmosphere in Washington. President Clinton has only himself to blame for the time, energy, and focus lost to the Lewinsky scandal. Those of us who were embarrassed by it and weathered it are not inclined to cut the president much slack on this.

For all the stress and late nights, however, I loved being in the White House. Friends used to ask me, sotto voce, "how's it goin'," as though I had cancer or some embarrassing rash. But the truth is that I always thought working in the White House was a privilege. And it was almost always fun.

One of the highlights was a White House visit by historian Stephen Ambrose, author of *Undaunted Courage,* and documentary filmmaker Ken Burns, who were collaborating on a PBS project on the story of Meriwether Lewis and William Clark and the expedition they led to explore the vast and newly acquired territories of the Louisiana Purchase. I was particularly tickled because Lewis had held roughly the same position for Thomas Jefferson that I held for Bill Clinton, working in the White House and even sleeping on a cot near his desk.

Ambrose and Burns had found relics of the expedition that had been locked in some Smithsonian closet for years and spread them over the floor in the room where Lewis used to work (or at least the room rebuilt on the room where Lewis used to work after the British torched the president's house in 1814): animal furs, stuffed birds, odd plants—the kinds of things a naturalist would haul back from the Oregon Coast by canoe, and that Thomas Jefferson would find fascinating. It was a history lesson, a reminder of how important what happened in the White House was, and—despite the irritants that took up so much time—what an honor it was to work there.

We were able to keep this country on a progressive course. We were still fighting for low-wage workers, children living in poverty, and people around the world who lived amidst deprivation, violence, and war—the people whose needs were at the core of our political beliefs. Working against two houses controlled by Republicans, the president achieved some major accomplishments on the economy, the environment, domestic policy, and foreign policy.

With this record, I believe Al Gore deserved to be elected, and indeed, I believe that he *was* elected. Had he been sworn in, the stage would have been set for an immediate engagement with the problems that, unfortunately, George W. Bush has ignored or exacerbated for almost eight years.

CHAPTER 6

George W. Bush
A Disastrous Conservative

As with the history of progressivism in America, there is a rich and substantive literature on the rise of the conservative movement in America. I will not try to retell this well-known story but instead will focus on what we know about conservatives' ideology after more than forty years of political advocacy and governing at all levels of government. The presidency of George W. Bush represents the clearest and most sustained application of this philosophy in action—and it isn't pretty.

The conservative framework rests on four propositions, each of which has been discredited over the past eight years:

- Supply-side tax cuts for the wealthiest are the best way to stimulate economic growth and ensure wide prosperity.
- Military might and preventative war are the surest way to exercise power legitimately and keep the country safe.
- Diversity in thought and lifestyle is a threat to the traditional family.
- Government is the enemy of a free people.

This worldview stands in clear contrast to the progressive vision I examined earlier. And unlike the tremendous successes that progressive ideas brought the country—victory in two world wars; the end of the Great Depression; full equality for women and African Americans under law; the rapid expansion of the middle class; conservation; and environmental, workplace, and consumer protections—conservative ideology as practiced by George W. Bush has translated into a series of dramatic failures that have divided the nation and threatened our security and reputation across the globe.

President Bush somehow managed to get almost all of the big challenges of the last eight years wrong. In the process, he helped to expose conservatism as an intellectually suspect philosophy incapable of handling America's most basic needs and pressing problems at home and abroad. Cleaning up this mess will take up an enormous amount of energy for the next president.

CONSERVATIVE TAX AND ENERGY POLICY

Echoing the supply-side approach of President Reagan (the one famously derided by George H. W. Bush as "voodoo economics" and renounced by Reagan's own budget director as a sham), President Bush has relentlessly argued for cutting taxes on the very wealthy as a means of producing economic growth. Unfortunately for the vast majority of Americans, the results of Bush's supply-side crusade have been no better than those of Ronald Reagan's failed experiment in helping those at the top with the argument that it will help those at the bottom.

Although there was moderate GDP growth in the United States through 2007, any gains in prosperity have been concentrated at the top and more than offset by indisputable declines in numerous other areas: median family income has gone down, the numbers of people in poverty and without health insurance have gone up, consumer prices are skyrocketing, the housing market is in shambles, and household debt is at an all-time high. At the same time, corporate profits are at record highs, wealth and income inequality has hit levels not seen since 1928, and crony capitalism is viewed as the normal course of business. In short, President Bush and conservatives have managed to take us back to the Gilded Age conditions that sparked the original populist-progressive uprising at the turn of the twentieth century.

Beyond its clear inequities and inefficiencies, Bush's tax policy also is causing a serious crisis by creating a federal budget deficit that threatens America's future prosperity. The Congressional Budget Office projects that the budget deficit for 2008 will be $357 billion (almost $195 billion more than in 2007), and this figure does not include the ongoing costs of war in Iraq and Afghanistan.[1] Worse still in terms of American sovereignty, foreign investors increasingly finance this debt as the dollar hit an all-time low against the Euro and America's trade deficit remains dangerously high.

Incredibly, the Republican standard-bearer in 2008, Senator John McCain, not only wants to extend Bush's tax cuts and extend the war but also has proposed more than $2 trillion (and climbing) in additional tax cuts, 58 percent of which will go to the wealthiest 1 percent of Americans and which will offer nothing—that would be zero—to middle-income earners.[2]

Perhaps this debt would be useful or sustainable if it was connected to new business investment, better jobs or higher wages, or new public infrastructure. But it isn't. Business investment is below that of the 1960s, job growth has been anemic, wages are falling instead of rising, and American roads, bridges, and transportation are in dire need of repair and expansion. In eight short years, conservatives under Bush managed to blow through a record budget surplus handed over from the Clinton administration and replace it with the highest deficits and one of the most inequitable and unproductive economies in our nation's history.

Of course, conservatives will tell you that their actions are built on sound truths that are quintessentially American. But in the hands of conservatives, ideas such as "economic liberty" and "personal freedom" simply dress up the servicing of the rich and powerful in the democratic garb of the Founding Fathers. Progressives dismantled this governing approach more than a century ago, but the bad ideas remain in vogue with conservatives. Not content to operate the tax code to the benefit of the richest Americans, conservatives also seek to dismantle the social welfare system created by progressives and replace it with private plans for retirement, education, and health care.

These privatization schemes will make lobbyists and select companies rich, but they won't do much to advance the interests of average Americans. Similarly, conservatives have created an aggressive corporatism that intervenes directly on behalf of powerful industries, regulates or deregulates to their liking, and fills the tax code with special set-asides and direct subsidies for favored interests.

Nowhere is conservative corporatism more apparent than in the Bush administration's approach to energy. From the rejection of the Kyoto Protocol to the subsidization of the oil industry to the editing of government papers in order to downplay the dangers of global warming, conservative energy policy has substantially set back efforts to create a sustainable economy and address catastrophic climate change. As with their ideas on taxes, much of conservatives' energy policy comes wrapped in the rhetoric of laissez-faire, sounding of "consumer choice" and "competitive industries," but is in fact little more than direct government support for an immensely powerful and profitable oil sector and a domestic extraction industry given leave to despoil some of America's most beautiful open spaces.

The conservative approach to energy over the past eight years has served as a vast transfer of wealth from citizens of all incomes (and from the natural resources that in fact belong to us all) to a relatively small band of oil industry executives and shareholders—a powerful modern echo of the Harding administration's management of the Teapot Dome oil reserve.

More of this same tax and energy agenda will not cure what ails America. Until conservatives come to grips with the fact that the status quo is not compatible with the public interest, they will continue to lose in the court of public opinion, set back our economy, and make a mockery of a democratic system that is supposed to represent the will of the people rather than a select few corporate interests.

THE CONSERVATIVE WAR IN IRAQ

It may seem difficult to top the sheer incompetence and extremism of Bush's economic program, but the formulation and execution of the war in Iraq might just give this domestic legacy a run for its money.

Before they first took office, George W. Bush and Dick Cheney promised the nation's armed forces that "help is on the way." Few pledges from the 2000 campaign today seem more hollow. In a few short years, Bush, Cheney, and Donald Rumsfeld eviscerated the readiness of the greatest military machine in the world. The U.S. Army is overstretched, overdeployed, and soon to be understaffed. The United States has been fighting in Iraq longer than it was engaged in World War II, with little or nothing to show for it beyond political instability in the region, continued violence, a diminished military, and a price tag for taxpayers estimated to be more than $1 trillion.

How did this happen? Contrary to popular belief among those who supported the war, liberals and conservatives alike, the failure in Iraq was not the result of failed execution, although there was plenty of that. The real failure was in the conservative vision—the flawed premise that the unilateral application of American military power in Iraq would create some kind of a positive domino effect in the Middle East and around the world.

In adopting the unrestrained internationalist rhetoric of President Wilson, President Bush and his cabinet seemed to ignore the fact that Wilson reluctantly entered World War I to defend America against German submarine attacks, to stop bloodshed in Europe, and to shape the postwar world through new forms of international engagement and institutions that could maintain the peace. U.S. entry into World War I was not the end result of a proactive gambit to use American military might to remake the world.

In contrast to Wilson's early restraint, President Bush diverted attention away from those who attacked us on September 11, 2001, to launch a premeditated war in Iraq built on manipulated intelligence and a politics of fear. Rather than attempting to stop the bloodshed in the region (as Wilson sought to do in Europe), Bush and his neoconservative advisers envisioned Iraq as the first war in a series of rolling battles to spread democracy through the region. Rather than building on the strong international support the United States enjoyed in Afghanistan, Bush willfully ignored, alienated, and misled the international community in an effort to steamroll opposition to the war. Colin Powell surely regrets his embarrassing attempt to cajole the United Nations Security Council into backing the war in early 2003 with phony data.

Bush did replicate successfully one aspect of the World War I experience—repressing civil liberties at home and engaging in a relentless propaganda effort to brand his opponents as traitors and appeasers. This historical parallel will not help his case, however.

The Iraq War is certainly the most visible failure of conservative foreign policy, but it was not the only one. On issue after issue, Bush and other conservatives have shown hostility and indifference to international rules of law and multilateral engagement that has caused a permanent stain on America's image abroad. Bush bucked the International Criminal Court, declaring that attempts to secure international justice and try war criminals violated American sovereignty. Then, instead of seeking international cooperation under the Kyoto Protocol, he reversed his own campaign pledge on global warming and said the United States would not work to reduce carbon emissions from power plants. Bush pushed for unilateral withdrawal from the Anti-Ballistic Missile Treaty in order to develop and deploy a ballistic missile defense system.

Bush's actions represented a broad assault on the post–World War II consensus that America's strategic interest rested on a multilateral foundation built on common purposes among democratic nations.

Conservatives also rejected the moral foundation of American foreign policy and global human rights by defending torture and arguing that the Geneva Conventions were "quaint" and "obsolete." An entire new generation of people across the globe now sees the United States not as a shining city on the hill or a beacon of liberty, but as a morally suspect nation that used Guantánamo Bay, Cuba, to eliminate due process for detainees and engaged in the abuses documented in photos at Abu Ghraib. These episodes—embraced and defended by many conservatives—will almost certainly harm America's interests, endanger American servicemen and -women, and damage its image for years to come.

Profoundly, the Bush administration squandered a unique opportunity after 9/11 to unite much of the international community against the real threat from extremists. As Pew and State Department world opinion surveys from 2000 to 2006 show, favorable opinions of the United States dropped considerably among key allies (from 83 percent to 56 percent in Great Britain, from 78 percent to 37 percent in Germany, and from 50 percent to 20 percent in

Spain) and in predominantly Muslim nations (from 75 percent to 30 percent in Indonesia and from 52 percent to 12 percent in Turkey).[3] The administration replaced international unity with a strategically and ethically challenged attack on a century of successful American efforts to defeat our common enemies while winning the hearts and minds of the world.

THE CONSERVATIVE ABUSE OF TRADITIONAL VALUES

The entire electoral strategy of George Bush and Karl Rove was built on the belief that traditionalist white evangelicals and Catholics would back the president as a man sent by God to liberate the home front from liberal relativism, criminalize abortion, deny equal rights to gay and lesbian citizens, and unite the country in a "war on terrorism" in the Middle East. In the process, these traditionalist voters would be expected to overlook the Republican Party's servicing of corporate interests and its pursuit of economic policies that would hurt these very same low- and middle-income voters.

As with any attempt to manipulate people's spiritual and religious lives for political gain, the effort failed on two fronts: it didn't represent the complex interests and beliefs of faithful citizens, and it turned off nearly everyone with its dogmatic attempts to transform narrow right-wing religious ideas into a governing agenda.

The Bush hope of realigning American politics with a base of ardent traditionalist voters did not always fit with the realities of a nation that is at once deeply religious and deeply tolerant of different views and beliefs. Bush scored many points with traditionalist voters for his anti-choice positions and appointments of John Roberts and Samuel Alito to the Supreme Court. But he lost just as many mainstream voters with his defense of torture and his unjust war in Iraq. Some faithful Americans credited him for standing up to "evil" after 9/11. But he lost many with policies that punished the poor and reneged on our stewardship of the planet.

Bush never seemed to grasp the complexity of faith in America; because of this confusion, he eventually turned off moderate and independent voters and sacrificed what the Reverend Jim Wallis calls the "moral center." In the end, it was difficult for Bush and the conservatives to claim the mantle of a religious presidency by advancing a hodgepodge of right-wing values.

Americans are a deeply faithful people, but most despise dishonorable attempts to manipulate faith for personal advancement and party politics. They also understand that not everyone shares the same beliefs and that you can't expect someone to respect your own values if you don't try to understand theirs—a lesson lost on the conservative moralists in the White House and Congress.

Nowhere were this hypocrisy and overreaching more apparent than in the conservative attempt to interfere in the end-of-life decision involving Terri Schiavo and her family. The conservative movement and Congress, then under the leadership of Tom DeLay, used the full force of the federal government (with the overt backing of the president) to insert itself into the personal decisions of a family and its doctors dealing with a difficult choice about the mental and physical state of their wife and daughter.

DeLay, incredibly, claimed that a woman he didn't know, who was in a persistent vegetative state, did not want to die and that, consequently, she deserved to have a court force her doctors to reinsert a feeding tube against the wishes of her husband. This was from a man who had earlier in his own life joined in a family decision to withhold dialysis from his ailing father. DeLay's statement against Michael Schiavo summed up this ethical obtuseness: "The sanctity of life overshadows the sanctity of marriage. I don't know what transpired between Terri and her husband. All I know is Terri is alive. . . .

And unless she had specifically written instructions in her hand and with her signature, I don't care what her husband says."[4] All of this was splashed across television for weeks along with self-righteous pronouncements from conservatives about the sanctity of life.

This gross violation of constitutional rights will go down as a shameful act of government interference in the lives of its citizens. The Schiavo episode will stand as a stain on conservatives and their attempt to reorder society and government along rigid, doctrinaire moral lines that most Americans reject as out of sync with their own religious values and the belief in religious pluralism enshrined in the First Amendment.

Hurricane Katrina and the Conservative Assault on Government

When conservatives aren't handing out tax breaks to people who don't need them or launching preemptive wars or telling people how to live their lives, they like to stand "on principle" against the encroaching state. The belief in limited government as a means of securing democracy and individual rights originated with America's liberal founders. Today's movement conservatives have managed to twist this sensible idea into a mantra built on the premise that government is always and everywhere the source of evil.

Despite overseeing the largest growth in federal spending on record, let's give George W. Bush credit on this score. Bush believes government is the problem, and he has done everything in his power to make this claim a reality. In eight short years, he has given us one of the most ignorant and just plain awful federal governments the nation has ever experienced. From doling out no-bid contracts to politicizing U.S. attorneys to putting mining and gas interests in charge of public lands, the Bush administration's handling of government has been criminally negligent and at odds with a commitment to the public interest.

The most infamous example of disdain for effective government is the tragic lead-up and response to Hurricane Katrina in 2005. Prior to the disaster, President Bush and the conservative Congress shifted funds for the maintenance and construction of levees in New Orleans to other programs. They neglected wetlands maintenance and protection in favor of servicing oil and gas interests in the region. The president stocked the bureaucracy with cronies such as Michael Brown, the former head of the Arabian Horse Association who was put in charge of the Federal Emergency Management Agency (FEMA), and David Safavian, the government's highest procurement officer, who was later convicted for obstructing a federal investigation looking into Jack Abramoff.

The lead-up to the storm in August 2005 was no better. Despite days of warnings from the weather services and state and local governments about the potential impact of Katrina, the Bush administration failed to aid or help coordinate evacuation efforts. Subsequently, thirty thousand people ended up in the Superdome with less than two days' worth of food and water. FEMA sent only one hundred buses to help evacuate people when seven hundred buses had been requested. As the levees were giving way under the onslaught of the storm, Bush attended a birthday party photo op for Senator John McCain and discussed his Medicare prescription drug plan. Defense Secretary Rumsfeld attended a baseball game. With New Orleans under a couple feet of putrid water, President Bush finally toured the area by plane and joined Department of Homeland Security secretary Michael Chertoff in proclaiming, "We are extremely pleased with the response that every element of the federal government, all of our federal partners, have made to this terrible tragedy."[5]

Nearly three years after President Bush declared in Jackson Square that "we will do what it takes, we will stay as long as it takes, to help citizens rebuild their communities and their lives," New Orleans is still reeling from a reduced population, decimated neighborhoods, rising crime, and inadequate public services and schools. This is perhaps not surprising. In the aftermath of the disaster, conservatives seemed more interested in blaming the victims of Katrina than rebuilding a great American city. Conservative radio host Glenn Beck proclaimed that the victims of Katrina were "scumbags," while former House Speaker Newt Gingrich noted "the failure of citizenship in the Ninth Ward, where 22,000 people were so uneducated and so unprepared, they literally couldn't get out of the way of a hurricane."

Hurricane Katrina revealed that when things go wildly wrong, there's no real substitute for the government. To their credit, legions of volunteers rushed to aid the hurricane's victims in New Orleans, Biloxi, and Gulfport. Millions of Americans sent financial and moral support. Many welcomed evacuees into their neighborhoods and homes. Great credit is also due to the Red Cross, the Salvation Army, and thousands of churches for doing what the government failed to do. These institutions temporarily revived the promise of Bush's "compassionate conservatism" and demonstrated the practical and moral value of faith-based institutions in times of disaster.

But despite the heroic efforts of citizens in the area and volunteers from around the country, Americans instinctively know that churches don't plug levees, deliver drinking water, or steer boats into swollen canals. Wal-Mart does not have its own private Coast Guard, and Sam's Club does not distribute MREs. Hurricane Katrina taught us that if you want to reduce government to a size where it can be "drowned in a bathtub"—in the words of conservative philosopher-king Grover Norquist—the first victims will be nursing home patients abandoned by those paid to keep them safe. Katrina also taught us that people who despise government have a hard time running it properly.

THE CONSERVATIVE ABUSE OF
CONSTITUTIONAL PRINCIPLES

From the moment this administration assumed office, it has been devoted to the persistent accretion of political power, freed from the restraints imposed by the separation of powers, scrutiny by the courts, oversight by Congress, accountability by the media, and any apparent sense of decorum, decency, or respect for our democratic traditions.

Power has, historically, always been exercised for its own sake, or to convey special privileges to special interests, but the project of the Bush administration will be remembered as something grander and far more pernicious than simply campaign contributions coming in and government contracts and corporate favors going out. They have acted, aggressively and unrepentantly, to undermine or overwhelm every possible source of countervailing power so that they could perpetuate their rule and operate with the freest possible hand.

They embraced the "unitary executive" legal doctrine as an excuse for ignoring the separation of powers ideal enshrined in our Constitution. Based on this obscure legal theory, the president has the power to act to protect our national security without oversight by Congress or the courts, much less legislation or court approval. It provides the administration's rationale for signing statements in which the president declares his intent to ignore a law he has just signed; for warrantless wiretapping and warrantless searches; for investigating library records and Internet search histories; for the "extraordinary rendition" and torture of suspected terrorists in Guantánamo Bay; and for the denial of habeas corpus to U.S. citizens and prisoners held in U.S facilities at Guantánamo and elsewhere.

Perhaps defensible when applied to decisions which must be made in an instant, at a moment of great danger, the Bush administration has carried the unitary executive theory far beyond the realm of national security, abrogating the Founders' vision of co-equal branches of government.

Beyond this overall framework, the administration has engaged in a number of additional acts that are constitutionally dubious:

- They stonewalled subpoenas and ignored treaties that had been approved by the Senate.
- They steered contracts to supporters and donors, blocked investigations of contracting abuses involving tens of billions of dollars, and appointed federal officials who acted corruptly.
- They rigged voting rights cases, tried to destroy their political opponents, and fired U.S. attorneys and replaced them with hacks and cronies.
- To stifle an independent flow of information, they muzzled and intimidated the press corps, held fake press conferences, used public money to pay for op-ed columns, censored government Web sites, and forcefully removed from scientific papers and government reports statistics and facts that contradicted their ideology or corporate interests.

What did this get us? Melting glaciers, the citizens of New Orleans abandoned, the relentless promotion of values that run counter to American culture (xenophobia, homophobia, creationism, and abstinence as the only permissible form of birth control), the greatest upward transfer of wealth in our history, our biggest deficits, $138-a-barrel oil, an unprovoked war that has cost us more than four thousand lives and more than $1 trillion, and a global image perhaps irreparably damaged by torture, rendition, and disrespect for international law.

Their complete contempt for public opinion and any check on their exercise of power was neatly summarized by Vice President Cheney. When confronted by the fact that 70 percent of Americans had turned against the Iraq War, he responded by saying simply, "So?"

"So," Mr. Cheney?

So much for a government that was of the people, by the people, and for the people.

PART THREE

Applying Progressive Values to Twenty-First-Century Global Challenges

Why America Is Poised for a
Progressive Revolution in Politics

The relevance and lessons of the original Progressive era for the challenges we face today could not be more vivid or clear.

From the 1890s to the 1920s, the United States experienced a renaissance in political thought and social activism that attempted to reconcile industrial capitalism with the nation's democratic ideals and the economic needs of its people. At a time when the prevailing conservative ideology served as an excuse for the lopsided accumulation of wealth and privilege, the original progressives answered a series of important questions about the direction of American life: How do we ensure that a growing economy does not exploit workers, endanger citizens, and undermine wider opportunity? How do we sever the connection between self-serving business interests and corrupt politicians? How should government be organized to better serve people and the national interest? What role should the United States play on the world stage?

The progressives' answers to these questions sparked legislative and political reforms that Americans today take for granted: the eight-hour workday, the end of child labor, the creation of workers' compensation, the direct election of senators, the referendum and initiative, the Federal Reserve, Social Security, safe food and medicine, national parks, and others. Looking overseas, progressive leaders

sought to build a lasting peace by creating a legal and security framework that protected us for a generation and helped to create a more
humane and just global order.

The circumstances we face today demand a new Progressive
era. Where progressives of an earlier era were called to solve problems on a national scale, this generation of progressives has been
called to restore America to its role as a global leader, not just mili-
tarily but morally. We need to attack problems that know no national borders, problems for which conservatism has proved that it
simply lacks the tools and the desire to solve. A global economy
that no longer accepts American preeminence, a security challenge
that cannot be solved unilaterally or with firepower alone, a climate that is changing in ways that will make earth more dangerous
and less habitable for billions of people—the scale of these challenges
is almost unimaginable.

How do we remake global capitalism for the betterment of
people everywhere without despoiling the whole planet or creating
an unaccountable class of financial elites? How do we defend our
people and our homeland against attack without pursuing a counterproductive militarism that undermines our security and alienates
other nations? How do we reform our government so that it serves
the interests of our people without turning into a deadening bu-
reaucratic state that is easily captured by corrupt interests?

In many ways, it was President Bill Clinton who pointed us in
the direction modern progressives should follow. Though his "bridge
to the twenty-first century" remains unfinished—and though the
Bush administration and conservatives have sought to weaken and
destroy it in their march backward in time—the foundations remain
solid and the principles that inform its vision remain in place.

First, as always, we should put families first, with policies that
allow Americans to keep their health, accumulate savings, assert

control over their own lives, and find fulfillment and self-confidence in the work they do. Second, our military and diplomacy must address the real security needs of the American people by reflecting the global trends that will shape our future, by recalibrating American power and realigning the instruments and institutions of U.S. foreign policy. Third, we must clean house and make government more open and transparent, so that it again works for the American people. Fourth, we need to reconnect our tax system to our own deep commitments to responsibility and hard work. And finally, as our faith and secular traditions—from Deuteronomy to the Gospel of Matthew to the Holy Qur'an to the Declaration of Independence—teach us, we must speak out for fairness, human dignity, and social justice in all our actions.

We have to think big, building on these pillars to tackle challenges posed by global warming, the global economy, and global security. We have to capture both Teddy Roosevelt's devotion to reform and Franklin Roosevelt's commitment to relentless experimentation, and we'll remember their greatest lessons: that progressives do our best work when we articulate concrete values grounded in the American tradition, clarify for the public what's at stake, measure progress by real results, and never lack the courage to challenge the status quo to find the real solutions to our problems that are consistent with our core beliefs.

- We need to transform our energy production and consumption patterns to encourage economic growth, job creation, and ecological sustainability.
- We need a more aggressive ethical and regulatory framework that pushes individuals and businesses to live up to personal responsibilities and corporate obligations to workers and communities.

- We need to improve our national economic development to encourage greater innovation and help all businesses and workers with better roads, transportation, urban renewal, high-quality broadband infrastructure, decent schools, and investment in science and technology.
- We need to strengthen existing international institutions, and move toward new forms of transnational security arrangements, to navigate better the cross-border challenges from terrorism, genocide, disease, global warming, immigration, and trade.

There are answers to these challenges, and it's our job to begin with the lessons and values of an earlier era and move from there to pursue political reform and economic justice on a truly global scale. The next Progressive era can set us on a path of progress to empower the broad masses of the American people, make families more secure here at home, and reestablish America as a moral leader at a challenging time in the history of our world.

CHAPTER 7

Solving the Global
Warming Crisis

The energy challenge we face in this new century is extraordinary in its urgency, its stakes, its scope, and its opportunity. Of course, energy has long been at the intersection of the economy, environment, and national security, and its availability and price have always been important factors in economic performance. Because energy has been produced over the past two centuries mainly by burning fossil fuels, dirty by-products soon threatened our air and water and spawned the modern environmental movement. Because critical elements of world energy supply come from unstable regions and hostile nations, energy has, for decades, played an important role in our national security.

But something different is afoot now. The realities of global warming and our growing dependence on oil, much of it imported, will make energy more pivotal than ever to our economic, environmental, and national security fortunes in the twenty-first century. The challenge we face is nothing short of the conversion of an economy sustained by high-carbon energy—putting both our national security and the health of our planet at serious risk—to one based on low-carbon, sustainable sources of energy. The scale of this undertaking is immense and its potential enormous.[1]

Americans, today, know they are living in an era of great energy insecurity. They are burdened by record oil and gasoline prices. Yet in the last few years, our addiction to oil has only increased. U.S. oil consumption is up 3 percent since January 2001, even though oil prices went up 314 percent during that same period. U.S. petroleum imports increased from 53 percent in 2000 to 62 percent of total consumption today. In 2007, we spent $331 billion overseas to buy oil—46 percent of our total trade deficit.

Inaction has left us dependent on unstable, undemocratic—and even hostile—regimes harming our ability to develop sound approaches to either oil-producing countries like Iran, Venezuela, and Russia or oil-consuming countries like China. Beyond the hemorrhaging of billions of dollars, our oil dependence leaves the American economy vulnerable to the vagaries of a wildly unpredictable international oil market.

But the security challenges of our oil addiction pale in comparison to the direct security and economic challenges posed by global warming caused by our dependence on fossil fuels. We are already seeing the environmental effects of global warming—extreme weather events, more intense hurricanes and cyclones, melting glaciers that are the primary source of fresh water for millions of people, increased heat- and flood-related deaths from Europe to India, declining coral reefs, and species pushed to extinction.

We will soon feel the national security consequences of global warming, including climate-induced human migration, increased food shortages, water insecurity, destructive weather events, the spread of disease, and increased competition for natural resources.

We will also feel the direct economic consequences of dramatically changing weather. According to the largest reinsurance companies, Swiss Re and Munich Re, the number of big weather disasters increased fourfold between the 1960s and the 1990s, economic losses jumped sevenfold, insured losses jumped elevenfold, and weather-related natural disasters are expected to double to $150 billion in the next six years. The 2006 Stern Review Report, commissioned by the UK government on the economics of climate change, estimates the economic damage of unchecked climate change at between 5 and 20 percent of GDP—between $700 billion and $2.8 trillion in the United States alone as crops wither, deserts spread, coastal areas are flooded, and new health and environmental challenges appear.[2]

The author of that report, Sir Nicholas Stern, the former chief economist for the World Bank, concludes that an expenditure of just 1 percent of GDP could mitigate the worst impacts of climate change, but environmental damage is still accelerating in the face of our inaction. Since the industrial revolution, the global average temperature has increased .8° C (about 1.4°F), and has been increasing at a rate of .2° C per decade since 1975. If the average temperature of the earth rises just two more degrees Celsius, the earth will be hotter than it has likely been in a million years, and our grandchildren could see extinctions on a massive scale, the melting of glaciers and ice caps around the world, and a significant rise in the sea level that may drive hundreds of millions of "climate refugees" inland from their coastal homes in places such as the Netherlands, Bangladesh, and America's Gulf Coast or across borders as the Sahara, Sonoran, and Gobi deserts spread.

The human costs and the greatest toll will fall heaviest on the world's poorest people—those least responsible but most vulnerable to climate change. Africa, for example, accounts for less than 3 percent of the global CO_2 emissions, but according to the United Nations Development Program, drought-affected areas in sub-Saharan Africa could expand by 60–90 million hectares, with dry zones suffering losses of $26 billion by 2060. Because of rising sea levels, desertification, dried-up aquifers, weather-induced flooding, and other serious environmental changes, between 150 and 200 million people, many living in some of the most dangerous places on earth—South Asia, the Middle East, the Horn of Africa—could be displaced by the year 2050.

That's why climate change, in my view, is the most demanding problem confronting America today; and why climate change commands a central space in the progressive agenda—because it lies at the crossroad of environmental, energy, economic, and security policies. Fortunately, a progressive approach to resolving the global warming crisis starts spinning a virtuous circle that can propel us toward more effective approaches to issues as diverse as energy and national security.

Swift action can head off the most disastrous consequences. And the solutions to the challenges of stopping climate change and creating a rational energy policy will be profoundly progressive, both in form and effect.

Our approach is rooted in progress itself—advances in technology and attitude that will allow us to break our addiction to oil and create a green, sustainable economy. And we are unafraid to use government as a catalyst to unleash the creative energies of American industry and dislodge the powerful interests blocking positive change.

Ending our dependency will vastly simplify America's security strategy by cutting the flow of funds to autocratic regimes in the "axis of oil" such as Russia, Saudi Arabia, Venezuela, and Iran. It will transform our relationship to the Middle East, the world's least stable region. It will inoculate us against economic blackmail by the Organization of the Petroleum Exporting Countries (OPEC). And it will slow the flow of money to terrorists, whether it streams through official Iranian bank accounts or is delivered in cash by wealthy sympathizers in other oil-producing lands.

Freedom—diplomatic, military, and economic—from oil obligations will allow us to focus resources on other challenges, building coalitions for peace and progress and attacking profound problems such as poverty and disease.

Battling climate change will have broad economic benefits for middle-class Americans and American industry as well. Every watt generated by a solar thermal plant east of Los Angeles or by a Montana wind field, and every joule with roots in a Minnesota biofuel refinery rather than a Middle Eastern oil field, represents dollars flowing to rural communities and thousands of small farmers, landowners, and investors in cooperative refineries and power plants. American coal in a power plant that captures carbon dioxide and sequesters it deep underground represents mining jobs that let blue-collar workers bring home the kinds of wages and benefits that have mostly migrated overseas, and the opportunity to export clean energy technologies to nations such as China (with the additional benefit of diminishing a carbon footprint that is now greater than our own). If Americans lead the world in green and alternative energy technology, we will find vast demand for our technology abroad and become more competitive here at home as we move to low-cost energy alternatives.

Progressives recognize that climate change is real, accelerating, and caused by humans—and that we must become the leader of the international effort to halt it.

We understand that the only way to deal with the costs carbon pollution is imposing on our society is to put a price on that pollution. The federal government has an obligation to impose hard targets for reducing greenhouse gas emissions and increasing consumption of energy from renewable sources. And we recognize that the federal government's policies will ensure compliance—where voluntary efforts are doomed to fail—and speed the shift to a greener economy while giving America's engineers and entrepreneurs plenty of room to do the heavy lifting.

Sustainable, green technology will transform our world as comprehensively as the Internet has done, touching almost every aspect of our work and of our lives. Just as the development of the Internet did, this transformative technology will arise from a partnership between government and industry. That partnership can begin and reach full fruition only with a commitment that comes directly from the White House to make the transformation of the U.S. economy a top priority (from a high-carbon to a low-carbon base)—a centerpiece not only of the president's energy policy but also of his or her economic program. This task is so encompassing that it will demand creation of a new National Energy Council in the White House, led by a national energy adviser whose mission will be the energy transformation of our economy and the promotion of these same steps abroad. Because our challenge is huge, full of opportunity and risk, the president will need the kind of single-minded attention that only a fully empowered national energy adviser can bring.

The debate about global warming is over. Despite the outright denial by some opponents and assertions by media outlets wishing to appear even-handed that the science is uncertain, the scientific community has decided otherwise. A 2004 analysis by Naomi Oreskes of more than nine hundred climate-related studies published in peer-reviewed journals found that not a single one disputed the existence of human-caused climate change.[3]

Climate change is real. Although a detailed energy policy is beyond the scope of this book, there is a broad, progressive strategy for reversing it by looking at the three most critical tasks before us: implementing an economy-wide cap-and-trade program for green-house gasses, transforming our transportation system, and overhauling the way we produce and consume electricity.

GREENHOUSE GAS EMISSIONS
CAP-AND-TRADE PROGRAM

To limit the rise in global temperature to approximately 2.0 degrees Celsius (3.6 degrees Fahrenheit) above preindustrial levels by 2050—"to keep the danger of intolerable and unmanageable impacts on human well-being" from becoming very high, as United Nations secretary general Ban Ki-moon recently noted—the United States needs to reduce emissions by at least 80 percent below 1990 levels by 2050.

In this instance the conservative laissez-faire model can't possibly work because of negative externalities—costs that are not captured by the market and passed on to consumers. The cost of burning fossil fuels for power does not reflect the costs of global climate change. Since it is not paying the full cost of greenhouse gas pollution, industry has no incentive to reduce it.

In this case, good economics—as well as sound environmental policy—demands that the government step in by regulating CO_2 pollution. There are two ways to regulate carbon across the broad economy—through a cap-and-trade program and through a carbon tax. Both approaches can work, if designed correctly. Both are cost-effective, market-based mechanisms and both could be imposed at the same point in the supply chain, for example at the mine or refinery.

The distinct advantage of a cap-and-trade program, however, is that it provides greater certainty with respect to the objective of limiting emissions. Designing a carbon tax would require policy makers to make an educated guess about the tax rate needed to hold emissions to the desired level. And factors such as the rate of economic growth would affect how successful the tax was in meeting its objective.

In contrast, a cap-and-trade system would identify the necessary level of carbon reductions, and then allow the marketplace to price the cost of those emissions, by auctioning off permits to emit. Uncertainty about the price of carbon credits can be reduced through provisions that allow companies to borrow emissions permits from later years or "bank" permits they didn't need in a given year, giving businesses more flexibility in meeting low-carbon emission requirements. And, employment of new low- and zero-carbon technologies will help reduce the overall cost of this energy transformation.

This "cap-and-trade" system was first used in the United States in the 1990s, where it has dramatically and cost-effectively reduced the amount of sulfur dioxide generated by coal-fired power plants. Europe already has a cap-and-trade system in place for greenhouse gas pollution, and a well-designed U.S. cap-and-trade system could be integrated into the European system and—ultimately—a global market for greenhouse gas permits.

Since overall emissions would be capped, a business that wants to increase the amount of CO_2 it emits beyond the amounts allowed under the permits it currently holds would have to buy permits from other businesses on the open market. On the other hand, companies that discover ways to cut emissions would be able to sell the permits they no longer need, earning a return on their efforts to cut back on greenhouse gas emissions.

Initial estimates by the Congressional Budget Office project that an economy-wide cap-and-trade program would generate at least $50 billion per year but could reach up to $300 billion. Revenues from the permit auction would be recycled back into the economy, easing industry transition with public investment in low-carbon infrastructure and technologies, job training, and tax incentives and ensuring that consumers, particularly low-income consumers, are not unduly burdened by potentially higher energy costs.[4]

Properly implemented, a cap-and-trade program forces industries to capture the real costs of their actions, but it will also spur creativity, reward ambition, and encourage the entrepreneurial spirit in the development of new, clean energy technologies.

TRANSFORMING TRANSPORTATION

To create a low-carbon transportation sector, we need to do three big things, and we need to do them simultaneously and in tandem with the introduction of a carbon cap-and-trade program. We must rapidly increase the fuel economy of our fleet of vehicles. We must push the development of low-carbon, alternative fuels alongside the requisite refueling infrastructure. And we must improve our public transportation infrastructure and city planning to reduce the number of miles we drive.

Highly efficient hybrid cars are becoming well established and increasingly popular in the United States. J. D. Power and Associates estimates that in the first six months of 2007, hybrid vehicles accounted for 2.3 percent of all new vehicle sales, and projects that by the end of 2007, sales of hybrids will be up 36 percent over sales in 2006 (a record 256,000 hybrids were sold in 2006).[5] Transportation policy should now be aimed at delivering the right incentives to more consumers and especially to our domestic manufacturers in order to increase dramatically the penetration of these and other fuel-efficient vehicles in the U.S. fleet.

The simplest and most effective step is to mandate better gas mileage. Fleet-wide average fuel economy in the United States peaked in 1987; since then the auto industry and its conservative allies have fought every effort to demand improvements, fearing for their SUV, light truck, and minivan revenue streams. The 2007 energy legislation raised fleet economy standards to 35 mpg, but that figure can and should be raised considerably higher—to 40 mpg by 2020 and to at least 55 mpg by 2030.

While there are a number of ways the auto industry might approach such a mandate, hybrid electric vehicles' growing share of the market shows great promise. Even more significant gains in creating a low-carbon fleet of vehicles will come as the next generation of hybrid cars, so-called plug-in electric hybrids, becomes widely available. A plug-in electric hybrid able to drive 20 miles on a single charge would get the equivalent of about 70 mpg; a plug-in capable of a 40-mile drive would get the equivalent of about 134 mpg at a cost equivalent to 75 cents per gallon of gasoline.[6] Robust government incentives should be deployed to hurry these clean cars onto our roads and highways. Chevrolet hopes to bring the Chevrolet Volt, a flex-fuel electric plug-in hybrid, to market in 2010.

We also need to change the way we fuel our vehicles and move to more sustainable low-carbon fuels. Recently, bioenergy has gotten a bad rap because of the U.S. reliance on corn to produce ethanol and the effect that diversion of the corn crop to fuel production has had on global food prices.

In 2006, U.S. ethanol production capacity was approximately 4.9 billion gallons—up 1 billion gallons from 2005.[7] Ninety-five percent of the ethanol produced that year was produced from corn, meaning 20 percent of our corn crop went into production but only satisfied 3 percent of our gasoline needs.

The rising prices of corn, soy, and wheat have sparked justifiable concerns regarding food price inflation. According to the U.S. Bureau of Labor Statistics, food prices went up 4.9 percent in 2007—the largest increase since 1990.[8] Food price inflation has been particularly tough on developing countries where commodity prices have jumped 40 percent in the past year.

The current reliance on corn-based ethanol is not sustainable economically or environmentally, and it is not the way biofuels are going to help meet our energy needs. We need to move away from corn-based biofuels to more sustainable fuels. Switching from corn to advanced biofuels made from switch grass, crop, and municipal waste can make a serious contribution to reducing CO_2, while relieving pressure on food prices.

Analysts at the Oak Ridge National Laboratory have concluded that the United States could produce enough biomass to replace more than one-third of our current oil consumption, while continuing to meet demands for food and livestock feed, if we move to advanced biofuels and increase agricultural yields.

A recent University of Minnesota study also suggests that mixed grasses grown on marginal farmland with minimal fertilizers and pesticides would produce 51 percent more energy per acre than corn grown on fertile land.[9] Moreover, the U.S. Environmental Protection Agency estimates that cellulosic biofuels would reduce lifecycle greenhouse gas emissions 80–90 percent relative to gasoline, compared to only 20–30 percent from corn ethanol.

Let me be clear: biofuels are by no means a "silver bullet" to all of our energy needs, but they certainly represent a piece of the solution. Bioenergy also holds enormous potential for poor farmers—especially for the two-thirds of the people in the developing world who derive their incomes from agriculture.

At the community level, farmers that produce dedicated energy crops can grow their incomes and grow their own supply of affordable and reliable energy, which can increase rather than displace food production. Cash and energy are key to increasing agricultural productivity in the developing world, and in turn to increasing food production.

But if we are going to use biofuels to help wean us from our oil addiction, we must grow them and use them the right way. If we are serious about a clean and sustainable energy future, we need to develop an appropriate regulatory framework to ensure that increased biofuel production does not compete with food production or lead to widespread deforestation and excessive use of water.

Finally, we need a new livable cities strategy that invests in more diverse and intermodal transportation networks, such as local mass-transit networks, regional and interstate long-distance high-speed rail systems, and green city programs that encourage the redevelopment of urban areas and reduce long commutes and suburban sprawl.

In our cities, too, we can promote denser, more desirable, and pedestrian-friendly neighborhoods by funding programs that redevelop abandoned and polluted urban lands close to transit networks—specifically by funding the expansion of the highly successful Brownfields program, which has brought much blighted urban land into vibrant and productive use. The low-carbon benefits of restructuring our cities are both short- and long-term. For example, if we construct over a million new homes every year based on new green home building standards, then the carbon impact could be profoundly long-lasting. Additionally, a recent study found that two-thirds of the buildings that will exist in the United States by 2050—homes, offices, and other non-residential buildings—will be built between now and then.[10] If 60 percent of this new growth were built using new compact land development patterns, this would reduce the need to drive by 30 percent and could save 85 million metric tons of CO_2 annually by 2030.[11] Rebuilding our metropolitan regions to promote new modes of transportation that in turn promote shorter commutes is ultimately a critical step toward creating a low-carbon economy.

Transforming the Way We Generate and Use Electricity

Electricity powers our homes, offices, and factories. Electricity for all purposes accounts for 36 percent of U.S. CO_2 emissions.[12] Burning coal produces 50 percent of our overall electricity, but 82 percent of CO_2 emissions from electricity. Natural gas and petroleum combustion account for the remaining 18 percent of emissions from electricity production.

As in the case of transportation, the road to low-carbon electricity is conceptually clear and consists of three basic elements: efficiency, renewable energy, and advanced coal technologies. While none of these steps is easy to implement, they also represent great opportunities for our economy and are far safer than another source of "clean" energy: nuclear power.

The easiest energy to save is the energy we never use. In California, energy efficiency programs have kept the state's per capita energy use flat since 1975, while consumption nationally has jumped 50 percent. We can work toward that type of performance nationally, beginning with a National Energy Efficient Resources Standard requiring electricity and natural gas distributors to meet a 10 percent energy savings threshold through efficiency upgrades and improvements in the grid. We should also allow small-scale generators of renewable energy to contribute to the grid, making it easier for thousands of small wind or solar energy producers to join in providing our electricity.

In addition, we can make significant gains by requiring efficiency upgrades in our appliances and our buildings, pushing through long-delayed but legally required updates on home appliance standards.

U.S. residences and commercial structures are woefully energy-inefficient, yet the $125 million authorized by Congress to help states adopt twenty-first-century, energy-efficient building codes has never been appropriated. Immediate action to codify widespread use of compact fluorescent bulbs (rather than incandescent bulbs), daylighting, solar heating and cooling, and more efficient appliances will allow a dramatic drop in energy consumption per square foot by then. The federal government should lead by example, adopting green building standards for its half million structures across the country.

Cutting consumption is a start. But, more than anything, we need to generate electricity in ways that don't allow carbon emissions into the atmosphere. And that starts with coal. In the United States alone, coal-fired plants that will produce about 145 gigawatts of new power are projected to be built by 2030, resulting in additional CO_2 emissions of 790 million metric tons per year. By comparison, annual U.S. emissions of CO_2 from *all* sources in 2005 were about 6 billion metric tons. And worldwide growth in CO_2 emissions from coal-fired electricity is expected to be almost ten times the expansion in the United States alone.

To maintain coal's viability as an energy source in a low-carbon economy, we must not only clean it of conventional pollutants that cause soot and smog, but eliminate the carbon dioxide pollution as well. The federal government should both price carbon emissions to reflect their true costs and speed development of the carbon capture and sequestration (CCS) technology that will allow coal-fired plants to operate while injecting carbon dioxide emissions underground for long-term sequestration.

Coal-burning power plants will, of course, be included under a cap-and-trade policy. As the cap falls over the long run, the increasing cost of emissions permits will push power companies to install CCS technology. But in the early years of a carbon cap-and-trade program, the cost of the permits is likely not to be high enough to spur the development of new coal plant technologies that capture and store emissions. Thus, operators will have no financial incentive to build clean plants for many years. A more effective way to guarantee that new coal plants are built clean is for Congress to mandate an emissions performance standard for all new coal plants. This standard would require all plants built after a certain date to have the capacity to sequester carbon and to begin actual sequestration a short time thereafter.

Such mandates are unsustainable without federal support, however. Although industry has some experience in injecting gasses below the earth's surface—the technique is used by oil companies to recover oil from deposits on the verge of being tapped out—we have much to learn about applying that technique to wide-scale carbon capture. While the Bush administration has been reluctant to fund demonstration projects, a study led by MIT's John Deutch and Ernest J. Moniz concluded that the U.S. government should take global leadership in large-scale demonstrations of the technical, economic, and environmental performance of large-scale integrated CCS systems.[13]

Although utilities will need time to adopt new technology and learn from the demonstration projects, the government will have to establish the new regulatory framework almost immediately and require that no new plants be built without low-carbon technology beginning in the very near future.

The United States has at least a two-hundred-year supply of coal within its borders along with abundant supplies of cleaner natural gas. A combination of regulatory directives and a real investment by the federal government in demonstration projects and new technology could allow us to use it without changing our climate forever.

But we also need to look beyond fossil fuels toward clean, renewable energy. Today, non-hydro renewable energy accounts for only
2 percent of our energy production. But the International Energy
Agency estimates that photovoltaic solar cells installed on rooftops
could ultimately meet more than half of U.S. energy demand. By some
calculations, large-scale concentrated solar thermal generation in just
seven southwestern states could provide seven times the total electricity being generated in the United States today—7 million megawatts.
Our country is also blessed by an abundance of other renewable
resources—in the winds across our oceans and our vast plains, in the
motion of the waves and tides, in the converted sunlight of plants, and
even in the heat of the earth—that are already being tapped on a small
scale but have massive room for expansion. Wind and solar generating
costs continue to decrease and are expected to fall by more than a
third by 2020. Some applications are already comparable in cost to
peak-demand conventional power costs, while the cost of coal, oil,
and natural gas is expected to rise.

Biomass is another encouraging source of renewable energy and
can generate electricity through various processes, including co-firing
biodegradable waste with coal in power plants. More than a hundred
such co-firing operations are up and running in the United States,
combusting methane captured from landfills, sewage treatment plants,
and livestock operations. Geothermal energy already generates enough
electricity to satisfy the needs of roughly four million people. Energy
can be harvested from waves and tides, and pilot projects are already up
and running.

We can begin to capture more of these resources by setting a
national renewable electricity standard, requiring states to generate
25 percent of their electricity from renewable sources by 2025.

In 2005, federal tax credits helped bring a record 2,431 megawatts of wind-generated electrical capacity onto the grid, making wind farms the nation's second-largest source of new power, after natural gas facilities. A recent Department of Energy report concludes that wind power could supply 20 percent of the nation's energy by 2030— displacing the amount of carbon produced by twenty million vehicles. The American Midwest has been called the "Persian Gulf of wind power," and offshore areas with favorable conditions could generate almost as much electricity as the nation generates today from all sources.

To help jump-start the industry to meet the growing demand, we need to provide consistent, long-term tax credits for renewable energy sources. State-level credits have been a major driver of wind power over the years. However, existing federal tax credits have been short-term and marked by one- and two-year extensions that have created uncertainty. These should be made long-term, and credits should extend to all alternative sources—not just wind, but geothermal, solar, and biomass as well.

BUILDING A GREENER ECONOMIC ENGINE

A progressive policy on climate change does more than mitigate global warming and lessen our dependence on foreign oil. Properly executed, it can bring new life to the American heartland and new jobs to America's industrial areas.

In the farm belt, creating cooperative structures for wind-generated electricity and biofuel production will put real money into farmers' and rural residents' hands. Tax credits and subsidies should be structured to support local ownership.

Analyses performed by the Apollo Alliance predict that biofuels and energy-efficiency investments could produce more than one million jobs in the U.S. economy by 2015. Researchers at the University of Tennessee predict that meeting the broader goal of "25 by '25" will create a staggering five million jobs and more than $700 billion of economic activity, while keeping a billion tons of carbon dioxide out of our air.

Increasing the share of renewable energy in the U.S. electricity system to 20 percent would create more than 355,000 jobs.[14] Low-carbon coal technology could mean 600,000 export jobs.[15] And though auto industry executives issue dire pronouncements about potential job losses now that CAFE standards are being raised and new technologies being encouraged, the truth is that car companies meeting the need for environmentally friendly vehicles are among the world's most profitable. And Detroit seems to have finally gotten that message. Taking the lead on flexible-fuel vehicles (which can run on either standard gasoline or on a biofuel blend) could mean 500,000 auto industry jobs over the next thirty years and serve as a lifeline for a depressed U.S. auto industry.

Annual revenue for solar power, wind power, biofuels, and fuel cells rose from $40 billion in 2005 to $55.4 billion in 2006, nearly a 39 percent increase in one year. Well-constructed incentives for research and purchase would help the United States compete against Japan and Germany, where government incentives have helped make those countries the leaders in solar energy technology, and against the European countries, which have captured 70 percent of the market for wind turbines.

On a broad scale, the federal government should mount a comprehensive effort to encourage research, investment, and training in technologies that will slow global warming, cut our dependence on non-renewable energy, and create jobs. The federal energy R&D budget should be at least doubled, providing direct expenditures to support basic science research, technology development and demonstration, as well as indirect financial incentives.

The government should also establish a quasi-public Energy

Technology Corporation to manage large-scale demonstration projects in alternative, low-carbon technologies that are not only technically feasible but commercially credible. And, with the shortage of skilled workers serving as a major barrier to expansion of clean technologies, the federal government should create a new Clean Energy Jobs Corps that can provide new pathways out of poverty, through service learning, and support for training and apprenticeship programs to help workers move into "green-collar" jobs in clean-energy industries that provide family-supporting wages and benefits.

The history of environmental legislation—despite opposition by conservatives at virtually every step—is a history of dramatic improvements in environmental quality at costs considerably lower than projected. Notwithstanding the achievements of Republicans like Bill Ruckleshaus, Russ Train, and Arnold Schwarzenegger, it is rare today to hear a conservative say that government mandates—intelligently mixed with incentives and research dollars—have unleashed the competitive genius of America's engineers and entrepreneurs to create solutions to pollution. At the same time, resistance to regulation has allowed the forces of the status quo to continue with business as usual.

All major carbon-emitting nations, including key developing countries such as China and India, will have to be part of the solution. In fact, most of the future emissions growth will be generated by developing countries that collectively will account for more than 75 percent of global emissions growth by 2030. But far-reaching, mandatory U.S. action has to come first. Without that, the United States will have no credibility to argue for broader global participation.

Slowing and reversing global warming is one of the greatest challenges in the history of humanity—a moral and political test of our will as a people. Failure will have extraordinary consequences not only for us but also for the earth itself and for the many generations to follow. Global warming offers opportunities as well as obstacles—new chances to tap the creative and entrepreneurial genius of America in ways that benefit both our environment and our economy. It is a challenge that progressives welcome because we believe it will bring out the best in our people and our nation.

The practical benefits that come with accepting our responsibility and embracing the opportunity to take part in this historic struggle are tremendous: ending our addiction to oil and weakening the hold terrorists and dictators have on our lives, strengthening the performance of our economy, creating new jobs, and improving the quality of our environment. The inspirational benefits are extraordinary as well: knowing that we are exemplifying the ideals that progressives have always stood for, including optimism, hard work, opportunity, innovation, and a moral commitment to all of humanity both present and future. The fight against global warming is not a fight that can be won by America alone, but it is a fight that can be won if America leads.

CHAPTER 8

Restoring the American Dream
in a Global Economy

During the last sixty years of the twentieth century, the American economy was impressive: GDP and productivity grew at a steady clip, standards of living rose, women and minorities were integrated into the workforce, more people obtained higher levels of education and became homeowners, America led the world in technology development, and its global financial strength was unrivaled. Programs and institutions as disparate as the GI Bill and the Marshall Plan helped our nation to create prosperity that was widely shared by Americans, while we also helped to expand opportunities for people abroad. Americans recognized that their own fate is intimately related to the fortunes of others, and we took steps to help strengthen other economies beyond our own. The two great features of this period of progressive economic strength were (1) expanding America's middle class and (2) showing economic leadership in the face of global change.

We are now entering an entirely new era. America's middle class is at risk and America is no longer the only powerful economic force in the global economy. At home, incomes are down, inequality is up, and economic opportunity is threatened. Technological change and global integration have fundamentally changed our situation but our policy makers have not offered a new strategy for the new world in which we live. Manufacturing jobs have moved steadily overseas, our public and private savings and investment rates are low, our dominance in science, technology, and innovation is threatened, and our fiscal imbalances leave us little room to tackle great challenges. China, India, Brazil, and other emerging economies are rising rapidly. Oil-rich nations and net exporting countries are sitting on growing reserves of American currency, allowing their sovereign wealth funds to invest more in our private economy. We've been weakened by Bush's domestic policy failures at home and by global developments over which we have no control. Most of all, we are weakened by the absence of leadership and the failure of policy makers to offer any strategy for the new conditions we face.

Rather than finding scapegoats abroad, decrying the rise of globalization or ignoring the new challenges we face, we need to once again harness economic change, as earlier progressives did, for the benefit of our own people and those around the globe. As we make a fundamental change in direction to save our climate, unhook our dependence on oil, and create an entirely new approach to energy to save our economy, we also must create an entirely new set of economic arrangements to support and expand the middle class, and restore economic mobility for American workers while also helping to improve living standards for the 2.7 billion people around the globe who still live on less than $2 a day, using new solutions every bit as creative and flexible as those conceived by our progressive forebearers.

Examining the state of the U.S. and global economies today, I see five interrelated challenges that progressives must address:

1. The current prospects for restoring vigorous economic growth are weak.

2. Our economy is dependent upon a high-carbon energy system, and global warming threatens to sap our economic resources.

3. The eroding American Dream leaves many of us fearful of the future, with few opportunities to get ahead, and little or nothing to fall back on in times of economic stress.

4. Globalization puts pressure on U.S. jobs while simultaneously leaving too many of the world's poor behind.

5. The Bush legacy of war spending and tax cuts for the wealthy leaves us with insufficient revenues to make needed investments in America's future, as we get closer to the time when aging baby boomers will demand more retirement and health resources.

A modern progressive vision for growth is uniquely suited to this time and these challenges. We need a strategy that meets our energy needs and ensures economic security and opportunity for our people, while also helping to improve the quality of life for millions around the globe through diverse but integrated policies.

THE ECONOMIC CHALLENGES TODAY

We need to accept the empirical reality that too many of our own workers suffer from economic insecurity and diminishing opportunities to get ahead in life. Nearly 50 million Americans lack health insurance. A declining share has employer-provided pensions. People are working longer hours than ever before, change jobs more frequently, and have more volatile incomes. Many have lost jobs to new technologies or foreign competition and the next job often will pay less. Fewer and fewer are represented by a union. Wages are stagnant despite a steady period of rising productivity (and rapidly increasing executive compensation). And costs are rising. Health care, housing, and child-care costs have risen steadily throughout recent years, but more recently energy and food prices have also skyrocketed. For example, gas prices in February 2008 were 66 percent higher than a year earlier. And consumer goods are rising in cost as well, as the dollar has reached new lows against foreign currencies.

To pay for these necessities, consumers have turned to debt, with average household debt at soaring levels, having reached a record 124 percent of average household income. Conversely, savings rates are at record lows.

All this insecurity limits a worker's capacity to take risks, like leave a job to return to school or start a business, and thus limits the opportunity to get ahead. Nor are we seeing rising levels of educational attainment as once we did. Thanks to changing demographics, our future workforce could well see the next generation be less educated than the people exiting unless current patterns change quickly. Too many of our schools fail to prepare our young people adequately for solid work or college education. More than half of America's 120 million workers (ages 25 to 64) have no postsecondary degree or credential of any kind. Fourteen percent of Americans (age 16 or older) have "below basic" prose literacy and 22 percent have "below basic" quantitative literacy. The American economy has fewer and fewer decent jobs for people with limited literacy, education, and training. The land of the American Dream now has less intergenerational income mobility than many other developed countries. Family incomes have risen on average within generations only because the incomes of women have risen as their participation in the workforce has grown dramatically; incomes of men have stagnated.

The net result of these pressures is an increasingly stratified society with a marked decline in social mobility. Economic inequality measured by the percentage of income going to the top 1 percent of

Americans is at levels not seen since 1928. Most Americans work hard, but many are unable to move up or even stay afloat. Consequently, too many Americans face needless frustration and hardship in an economy that produces nearly $14 trillion annually in goods and services. This is both economically inefficient in terms of the productive capacity of our citizens and morally suspect in terms of our nation's democratic promises and its commitment to advancement for all people.

After several years of growth that was weak by historical standards, the economy has slowed to a crawl or even recession and prospects for vigorous recovery are weak. We cannot continue to rely upon the engine of growth in the Bush years. The housing bubble, built on weak regulation and cheap credit, had to come to an end. Similarly, our economy can no longer get by on consumption that is heavily subsidized by debt. And productivity rates must increase if we are to achieve long-term growth. Economists estimate that our standard of living doubles roughly every quarter century with productivity growth of 3 percent annually, while it takes almost seventy years to double living standards at a 1 percent productivity growth rate.[1] Our current patterns are not reassuring: productivity gains fell below two percent in 2005, 2006, and 2007—the biggest drop since the productivity boom of the mid-1990s.

Globalization and technological changes have surely contributed to these disruptive patterns. But the decline of unions and federal policies that aid the wealthy and well-connected at the expense of the middle class and national needs are also to blame. There's no question that this domestic neglect must be addressed, particularly in terms of building a viable twenty-first-century social opportunity platform that provides people with the economic security to navigate the turbulent world economy. Beyond domestic concerns, a new progressive economics must recognize the collective needs of people across the globe and should resist the temptation to fall back into the false premise that we can and should take care only of ourselves. In fact, as standards of living rise around the globe, we create new markets for more American goods and services. Core progressive values and the realities of an integrated world economy demand that we strive for economic betterment for all people, not just our own. Put simply, we rise or fall together, both at home and abroad.

How do we solve all of these challenges simultaneously?

A New Direction: Long-term Growth Through Education and Innovation

To achieve the energy transformation outlined in the previous chapter, and to advance America's economy more broadly, we need a strategy built on innovation: greater investment in research and development, science and technology, a more successful system of lifetime education starting in preschool that provides graduates and workers with degrees and credentials of economic value, and strong alignment of national policy with national economic needs.

The energy transformation will require direct investments from both the private and public sectors and a renewed federal commitment to innovation, science, and technology. The key to this innovation transformation lies in new investments and focus on human and physical capital—to boost productivity, transform our system of education, and reinvigorate innovation in technology, engineering, math, and other creative arts and sciences.

We must work to develop a smarter, more creative, and more flexible workforce by reengineering our education and job training system. Education must be seen as a continuum from early childhood development to secondary school, post-secondary credentials, adult learning, and workforce training. Given the numerous empirical studies documenting the essential role of early education in the future development of young people, universal preschool must become a national priority as we seek to build the next generation of citizens and workers. For those currently in primary or secondary school, we need to improve achievement through increased learning time and better teachers, and ensure that more students are ready and able to attend college.

To start, we need to be honest with ourselves. Years of well-intentioned but ultimately insufficient reforms have only been able to nudge overall academic performance in our nation's public schools.

Despite steps to increase per-pupil spending, decrease student-teacher ratios, strengthen standards, and recruit a better-prepared teaching force, student test scores have remained stubbornly flat over the past thirty-five years. By international standards, the United States spends far more than other nations on education yet receives far less value in terms of educational outcomes. Too many of our schools are turning out kids who lack the basic skills and knowledge to enter college or compete economically.

We know that teacher quality has the biggest impact on student achievement. Studies consistently show that effective teachers do the most to help students learn, while the negative impact of inexperienced and out-of-subject teachers on student performance is also well documented. A very good teacher as opposed to a very bad one can make as much as one full year's difference in the achievement growth of students. Dramatic increases in student learning will therefore require better teacher preparation programs, well-designed professional development opportunities, good working conditions, and the creation of non-traditional teaching paths.

In order to attract the best talent to teaching, we also need to improve starting pay for teachers. Similarly, career advancement opportunities and financial rewards are proven methods of motivating employees in every profession, and we should do more of this for teachers and principals, by implementing pay for performance salary structures, and giving salary incentives for hard-to-fill subject areas and hard-to-staff schools. As we increase salaries for starting teachers and other career opportunities, we also have a duty to find more effective ways to remove teachers who are not serving our kids well.

Steps to encourage innovation and experimentation in our school systems will also be critical to breaking the status quo and finding new ways to tackle seemingly intractable problems. This includes ideas such as small learning communities, early enrollment in college-level courses for credit, youth apprenticeships, charter schools, and online learning. As long as new institutions and programs are held accountable for academic results, they should have maximum flexibility to try new ideas. If successful, these ideas should be replicated elsewhere.

Expanded learning time is another avenue that often gets overlooked in reform discussions. Our school year is organized for the late-nineteenth-century economy, not that of the twenty-first century. Summer learning loss is a well-documented occurrence for American students and is particularly harmful for low-income and minority students, who often lack the enriching out-of-school experiences that their wealthier peers enjoy. A reformed school calendar, more time on task, enhanced tutoring, quality after-school programs, and experiential learning—these are all opportunities that can be especially important for disadvantaged students.

The role of higher education remains a key priority for maintaining America's competitive advantage and leadership in science and technology. With China building a hundred new research universities, and India reevaluating its own national higher education strategy, we cannot expect to remain an economic superpower with educational investment lagging.

According to the Department of Education, more than 80 percent of the fastest-growing jobs in the United States require some form of post-secondary education. However, numerous comparative studies have concluded that the United States is falling well behind other nations in its ability to prepare our students properly for higher education and the new economy.

A 2003 UNICEF report ranked the United States eighteenth out of twenty-four nations in terms of the overall effectiveness of its national education system.[2] A 2005 report by the Organisation for Economic Co-operation and Development ranked the United States ninth among industrialized nations in the share of its population with a high school degree, and seventh in terms of those with a college degree. Twenty years ago, the United States ranked first on both indicators.[3]

While a four-year degree may not be for everyone, some kind of post-secondary credential is necessary in order to compete in the global economy. There are four overarching principles that should guide any progressive policy on higher education: first, everyone should have access to some kind of higher education and the opportunity it affords; second, we have to raise high school graduation rates; third, we must ensure that students have not just access but a chance to succeed in higher education and earn credentials of economic value; and finally, higher education policy must be more closely aligned with our nation's economic and societal needs.

To begin, we must ensure that every American student who wants to go to college—and does his or her part to qualify—can afford higher education. This is not the case today, as nearly 25 percent of academically qualified low-income students either do not apply to college or drop out because they are unable to keep pace with escalating prices. Next, we must ensure that all students are adequately prepared for the challenge of higher education so that college or a post-secondary credential is a realistic option if they so choose. Even among those who enter some kind of college, the drop-out rate is about 50 percent. Students need more preparatory courses to ensure that they are college-ready and, once they get there, educational institutions that better meet the needs of today's students, many of whom are working.

We also need to address the crisis of college funding. At a time when university endowments are exploding in value, the average student borrower now graduates with $27,600 of debt—almost three and a half times what it was a decade ago. And this does not take into account the increased debt burden on parents, as middle-class parents have increasingly taken out second mortgages and home equity loans to pay for their children's higher education.

We also need to increase and improve lifelong learning opportunities for those currently working so that people can stay employable. We need new incentives for employers to invest in the credentialed and portable education of their employees both for basic skills and post-secondary training. And we need to provide stronger financial incentives for working adults to invest in their own education. We should also use existing national service programs such as Ameri-Corps, and invest in new ones, to help train people for future work while also tackling national challenges such as increasing health-care services and reducing greenhouse gas emissions.

While addressing the needs of students, we must also attend to the needs and goals of our economy. American economic competitiveness should be seen as a vital function of our K-12 and higher education systems. While the exact shape of the future is impossible to predict, it is possible to plan for it; we know the general contours of what the future will require. For example, it's no surprise that our nation needs more engineers and scientists. We know that there are huge social problems that may ultimately be solved through technological advances—issues such as global warming, environmental sustainability, and disease treatments—and these fields merit major investments in study, research, and building markets for these technologies. We also know that with the aging of the baby boomers there are imminent shortfalls in a range of health care occupations. We should insist that education institutions engage with employers to ensure that students graduating from high school and with a post-secondary degree or credential are ready for jobs in the modern economy. Indeed, forward-minded employers increasingly realize that they too have a vital stake in a higher education policy that is better connected to our national economic goals.

Finally, we must recognize that America's capacity to be a leader in innovation depends upon the talents, skills, and spirit of the entire U.S. workforce, which currently includes 25 million people, who are foreign-born workers who immigrated to the United States temporarily or permanently.

Just like my grandparents, foreign-born workers contribute to America's success, but today our immigration system has broken down. We need to be tough and smart to get our immigration system under control. It is unacceptable to have twelve million people in our country who are outside the system. We must require illegal immigrants to become legal, and reform the laws so this can happen. They should register for legal status, pay their taxes, learn English, and pass criminal background checks if they want to remain in the country. Those who have a criminal record or refuse to register should be deported. We also need stronger border security and tougher penalties for corporate employers that hire illegal immigrants.

Current policy also makes it difficult for the "best and brightest" to study, work, and start a business here, so we also need to allow U.S. educational advance degree students to remain in the U.S. workforce after graduation, adjust export and visa control policies to make scientific exchange easier, address the backlog of applications for employment-based visas, and develop an entirely new, fairer temporary worker visa program that can help to meet short-term needs of employers without doing damage to domestic U.S. workers. A diverse, talented, and committed American workforce is an essential component of a strategy to establish an economy based on innovation.

NEW SECURITY AND MOBILITY FOR AMERICAN FAMILIES

As we work to shape the macroeconomy through energy transformation and investment in innovation, we must also directly confront the economic insecurity and declining social mobility of America's great middle class. Only through basic economic protections, such as health care and retirement security, and social mobility tools, such as education and access to wealth building, can people take full advantage of the opportunities generated by a growing economy.

America's global economic leadership over the last century was greatly enhanced by our systems of public education, Social Security, employer-based health care and pensions, unemployment insurance, and home ownership incentives including VA and FHA loans and the home mortgage tax deduction. These progressive solutions provided a framework for a competitive domestic marketplace, worker mobility, and health and financial security. Unfortunately, our system of shared responsibility no longer provides the financial base it once did, and it needs to be rebuilt.

In order for Americans to prosper in the global economy they must be healthy, they must have appropriate technical and creative skills, they must be financially literate, they need some measure of financial security, and they need to be able to build skills and assets throughout their lifetime. The core of this new social opportunity platform must be high-quality, affordable health care, coupled with good-paying work and increased opportunities to build wealth through retirement savings and sustainable homeownership done right.

Quality, Affordable Health Care for All

In order to extend basic health care protection to all Americans quickly, we should provide guaranteed access to health coverage through any one of the following means: employer-sponsored insurance, Medicare for seniors, Medicaid, or private coverage purchased through a new group insurance pool modeled on the Federal Employees Health Benefits Program, that includes a Medicare-type option. The new national insurance pool will offer the cost-saving benefits of group purchasing to individuals who do not today have access to this cost-effective strategy for purchasing health coverage. It will also help small businesses and other employers who have trouble finding group coverage by establishing new, affordable options for these employers.

In return, everyone would be expected to enroll in coverage; if they choose not to enroll, they would pay an income-related charge for the insurance on the care they would invariably need. New subsidies—through expanded Medicaid eligibility and refundable tax credits for those purchasing private coverage—will make coverage more affordable for all. No family should pay more than a small percentage of its income for insurance that provides quality, affordable health care. New technologies, an increased focus on prevention, and research on the effectiveness of treatments will improve the quality of care and reduce overall costs.

The United States spends more on health care than any other nation. In 2003, U.S. health care spending totaled $1.7 trillion, which is an average of $5,670 per person.[4] Yet Americans do not always receive the best-quality care. In fact, American adults receive recommended care only about half the time, with underutilization more common than overutilization. The United States ranks twenty-eighth in the world on infant mortality; thirty-first in life expectancy.

The mismatch between what we spend and what we get, in terms of the uneven quality of health care, presents a crucial challenge in achieving affordable, appropriate health care coverage for all. It is not enough merely to expand access to the current system. Americans must also secure better value for their health care dollars through improved health care quality, outcomes, and efficiency.

First, we must create a national focus on disease prevention and health promotion. The United States is plagued by preventable diseases that have a devastating impact on personal health and contribute to the nation's soaring health costs. Yet our current health system focuses on treating these diseases after they occur, rather than promoting good health and reducing the incidence of disease in the first place. This misguided approach is due, in large part, to disincentives embedded in the system. With no guarantee that an enrollee will remain in a specific insurance plan, insurers have little incentive to invest in keeping that enrollee healthy over an extended period of time. Instead, they simply try to avoid enrolling people who are, or are likely to become, sick. To ensure that these failings are not perpetuated, my colleague, Dr. Jeanne Lambrew, and I have proposed the creation of a Wellness Trust, to set national prevention priorities and to employ effective delivery mechanisms including traditional health-care providers, but also extending prevention activities outside of traditional settings to schools, workplaces, and pharmacies.[5]

We must also greatly increase our understanding of what constitutes high-quality care. Most health research focuses on determining whether a particular medicine or treatment is safe and works. There is little credible information comparing the relative value of different treatments. As a result, patients often receive care that drives up costs without improving health outcomes. Federal investment in research on the comparative clinical value and cost-effectiveness of available treatment options will enable patients, providers, and payers to make sensible health care choices.

Finally, we must bring health care out of the information "dark ages" and deliver critical information when and where it is needed. While doctors' offices and hospital rooms whir with exciting new medical technology, information technology is largely absent. Medical equipment churns out volumes of information, most of which is reduced to paper and stuffed in files along with handwritten notes. Cutting-edge information technology, structured to safeguard patients' privacy, has the potential to dramatically improve health care quality and produce a better care experience, while reducing total health care costs through administrative and clinical efficiencies.

To help oversee and rationalize the overall process of cost containment, Senator Tom Daschle, my CAP colleague and friend, has proposed creating a new Federal Health Reserve (Fed-Health), modeled somewhat on the Federal Reserve System. Fed-Health would be composed of a panel of Senate-confirmed experts— doctors and clinicians, health benefit managers, economists, and researchers—that would "assess the health impact and cost effectiveness of major and/or costly services . . . vote on recommendations on the ranking of such services to set model coverage and cost sharing policy . . . [and] set processes for exceptions to these rules and separate policies for vulnerable populations."[6] It would take the politics out of how we finance medicine, and while it would not regulate the private sector, it would use tools, primarily benefit rankings, to guide best practices and protocol to make sure taxpayer dollars are spent wisely and on the best care.

Change of this magnitude will not come on the cheap. Progressives committed to universal health care need to ensure that expanded coverage is paid for in an equitable and sustainable manner. We all need to do our part. While we can achieve considerable overall savings from rationalizing our health care delivery system and emphasizing cost-effective treatment strategies, it will still cost money in the short term to provide quality, affordable coverage to every American. Although there are a number of proposals to pay for expanded coverage, I have proposed a broad-based mechanism to fund the necessary investments: a small value-added tax whose revenue is exclusively dedicated to improving the health system. A value-added tax (VAT) is a tax on the value of a good or service added in its various stages of production—effectively the difference between what a business buys from other businesses and what it sells. A broad-based VAT of 3 to 4 percent with targeted exemptions (for example, exempting small businesses, food, education, religion, and/or health care) will be sufficient to offset the rough annual federal cost of the health care reforms—estimated to cost around $100 billion per year. Revenue from the VAT will go to a trust fund and be used exclusively to finance the plan.

BUILDING WEALTH

As we work to extend health care to all Americans, we must also focus on ways to increase the ability of more Americans to get and keep decent-paying jobs and build and sustain wealth over the course of their lifetimes. The process of wealth building requires steps to ensure that people's current work actually pays a decent wage and offers real benefits. People shouldn't face barriers to joining unions, both as a democratic right and as a means for bargaining for fair wages and just benefits. When unions are strong and able to represent the people who want to join them, wages and benefits increase for workers throughout the economy and that's why it is vital that Congress strengthen the right to organize and form a union. In addition, the minimum wage needs to be increased substantially and pegged to inflation. The Earned Income Tax Credit should be greatly expanded to help low-income families remain in the workforce without falling into poverty.

Wealth building and economic security also mean giving people secure places to put their paycheck and responsible lending options that don't charge people interest in the hundreds of percentage points (as some payday lenders do today), protection against racial discrimination and predatory subprime lending, and viable home mortgage options on fair and sustainable terms. It also includes ensuring people a secure and dignified retirement through a universal 401(k) system, as well as improved protections for home ownership.

BUILDING A GLOBAL MIDDLE CLASS

In taking these steps to shore up the security and opportunity of our own citizens, and to create new markets for our own goods and services, we also must develop a new approach to both poor countries and more vibrant, emerging middle-income countries that continues America's longstanding commitment to helping others to lift themselves up by focusing on ways to build a thriving global middle class. Ensuring that the benefits of globalization are as widely shared in nations abroad as we want them to be here at home could create a race to the top where rising standards of living and greater economic integration and trade reinforce each other.

If we are smart and strategic, America need not fear the rising economic clout of emerging economies like China and India. If we get our domestic house in order, insist on rising consumer safety and core labor standards, and work with the international community toward monetary and macroeconomic reforms to unleash domestic consumption and reduce foreign trade surpluses, these countries could emerge as powerful markets for our high value-added products and restore trade and payment balance. For the least-developed countries, we need to focus on helping them create their own productive capacities and institutions so that over time they, too, can join the world's developed economies.

To this end, we need to refocus the three main elements of international economic policy—trade, aid, and monetary policy—on twin goals of global growth and increased living standards. This policy agenda would need to differentiate between countries at different levels of development.

To start, we should bolster the "decent work" efforts of the International Labor Organization—an agency created at the end of World War I to encourage economic harmony among businesses, governments, and labor organizations and to ensure that the world's workers were treated humanely. Similarly, we must also ensure that projects funded by the World Bank and financial stabilization strategies recommended by the International Monetary Fund promote the kind of development that provides a decent standard of living for the largest number of people.

The goal of a progressive decent-work agenda is to promote a world economy where more people can afford to buy the products and services they create and more people have access to cheaper and better goods. This is not rocket science. Henry Ford pioneered this idea in the early twentieth century by raising wages for his workers to $5 a day so they could more easily buy the cars they were helping to produce. With more people buying Model T's, Ford could lower prices and still make money. Rather than promoting social unrest and division, a global decent-work agenda focuses on building a rising class of economically stable and secure citizens committed to ongoing peace and prosperity.

Promoting decent work will require a combination of carrots

and sticks. We should help countries with financial and technical assistance, but we should also insist that in return for increased access to our markets these countries make progress toward creating a middle class. For some countries we will work to ensure that their laws are enforced; we will provide others with expertise to help build social safety nets; for still others we will directly invest in infrastructure. Promoting decent work will require a more integrated approach to our trade and foreign policy and must involve integrated efforts from international institutions, foreign governments, businesses, and civil society organizations.

PAYING FOR WHAT WE NEED

Any discussion of a new progressive economics must make fiscal responsibility a central operating principle rather than a mere rhetorical device. The cumulative U.S. national debt stands at roughly $9 trillion today and is only getting worse because of the Bush administration's current path of tax cuts, runaway deficit spending on misplaced priorities, and a weak dollar. The nation's debt, in turn, makes it difficult to address the long-term challenges of entitlement programs such as Medicare and threatens the new progressive investment agenda that will be necessary to make the transition to a low-carbon, high-innovation economy. In short, progressives must be serious about paying for our investment priorities and ensuring that economic growth is backed by fiscal rectitude.

Tax reform that creates a fair, simple, pro-growth and pro-work tax system should be a top priority. Under our current tax system, the incentives for good behavior and outcomes are turned upside down. Rather than allowing CEOs to pay a lower tax rate than their administrative assistants, we should tax income derived from work (the basic paychecks most of us get) and income derived from capital (the stock options that many CEOs and investors receive as compensation) at equal rates. Rather than subsidizing polluters and the oil and gas industries, we should put a price on carbon and reinvest this money in completing the transformation to a low-carbon economy.

Closing loopholes and enhancing tax enforcement can maintain essential fairness in our tax system. To ensure greater progressivity in the tax code, we should eliminate the cap on the employer side of the Social Security payroll tax and reform the estate tax by setting the exemption and marginal tax rate at 2007 levels, indexing the exemption for inflation, and making the law permanent. Under this reform, only a tiny fraction of the very wealthiest estates would be subject to the tax.

By accepting the fiscal reality that we need sufficient revenues to meet our national priorities and to provide a platform of social opportunity for all, we can begin correcting the imbalances and excesses of the past eight years. Furthermore, the ideas outlined in this chapter can be achieved while still keeping government revenue as a percentage of GDP to an average of 19 percent over the next ten years—consistent with the levels during the economic expansion of the Clinton administration.

This path of economic growth, economic opportunity, and just distribution of the nation's wealth was forged by the great progressive leaders of the twentieth century to help create the largest middle class in world history. As progressives today face the challenges associated with climate change, rising inequality, and declining social mobility, it is essential to update this framework to build an equally successful twenty-first-century America.

CHAPTER 9

Creating Sustainable Security for America and the World

My colleague, CAP senior fellow Gayle Smith, has put forth a useful framework for understanding global policy called "sustainable security"—the integration of necessary national security means to protect Americans from physical harm with a wider social focus on "human security" to create a world that is more just and stable and lives up to FDR's four freedoms, a world where poverty, threats of violence, and political repression are replaced by economic opportunity and freedom. Smith describes the goals of this framework as follows:

> By complementing the traditional concept of national security with human security, America can craft a strategy that is more sustainable for the simple reason that it would afford the possibility of dealing simultaneously with short-term, nation-state-based threats and the global challenges that transcend state borders. But getting there requires three core elements: an organizing principle that can unite a majority of the world's people; the elevation and strategic utilization of the full range of our foreign policy tools; and a revitalized international system that reflects not just the challenges that existed when it was created in the wake of World War II, but also the realities of today.[1]

The reality of global affairs demands that we make these three conditions a primary focus of our efforts. American leaders survey a dramatically different landscape than those who shaped foreign policy in the past. There is no Nazi Germany, no imperial Japan, no Soviet Union, and no great ideology to challenge the United States. Instead, transnational challenges that cannot be confronted or overcome by traditional military means have fragmented the security environment even as globalization has bound the world more closely together. Terrorists, rogue regimes, the proliferation of weapons of mass destruction, environmental degradation, poverty, and disease have replaced wars between major powers as the greatest threats to international peace and security.

America's might and prosperity are unmatched. The United States spends more on defense than every other country combined, and we produce 20 percent of all global economic output, just slightly less than the combined output of the twenty-five nations in the European Union. By these measures, America is undoubtedly the world's sole superpower. In the modern world, however, unsurpassed military and economic power alone does not necessarily translate into sustainable security for our country or the world.

A new approach must recognize the changing threats of the twenty-first century and utilize the power of progressive values grounded in democracy, self-determination, economic opportunity, human rights, and humanitarian support. It must recognize the decentralized nature of the threats we face. It should not hesitate to use force as necessary, but it should recognize the ineffectiveness of traditional military force alone and the increasing need for international cooperation in war and in peace within a framework of international law. It must start with a resolution of the conflicts in Iraq and Afghanistan, and go forward with the knowledge that it is easier to prevent a crisis within a framework of international collaboration than to extinguish a crisis once it is burning.

A progressive strategy of sustainable security must start by firmly rejecting the faulty and counterproductive "war on terror" frame that has led to disastrous policies since 9/11. Terrorism is a tactic that can be employed anywhere, not an ideology like communism that is embodied in a powerful state. Fighting al-Qaeda is not at all like fighting Hitler or Stalin. The mentality of believing we are waging "World War IV"—as neoconservative writer Norman Podhoretz has dubbed it—has caused many of the problems we face today.

The war in Iraq proves even a solo superpower does not get to dictate world events. So we must begin to look beyond Iraq, to recognize the changing nature of the threats we face. There always will be rogue nations whose strength and belligerence make them a danger to us and to the world. North Korea's history of violence and repression and its acquisition of nuclear weapons make it a clear threat to international security, as does Iran's support of terrorist groups and pursuit of nuclear capabilities in the face of international opposition.

Although the explosive development of East and South Asia does not necessarily herald the arrival of China, India, or any other nation as a military power on the level of the United States, we remember Paul Kennedy's observation in *The Rise and Fall of the Great Powers* that these aspects of power are usually intertwined and that military and political power can easily flow from economic strength.[2]

Threats to U.S. national security in the twenty-first century will arise not only from sovereign states but also from every corner and crevice of the globe. In 1997, Russian general Alexander Lebed revealed that one hundred Russian suitcase nuclear weapons were unaccounted for.[3] Osama bin Laden has said it is his duty to acquire nuclear weapons. The stage is set for what Graham Allison calls "the ultimate preventable catastrophe," a nuclear weapon in the hands of a terrorist group. Weak and failing states provide homes for these blights on the international community, serving as incubators for transnational threats.

From Somalia to the tribal areas of Pakistan, the lack of effective governments across large swaths of the less-developed world poses a tremendous risk to the United States. We can no longer be indifferent to "a quarrel in a far away country between people of whom we know nothing."[4] In addition, we face new threats as diverse as oil dependence, global warming, and the spread of global disease like severe acute respiratory syndrome (SARS), tuberculosis, and HIV/AIDS. Each of these problems brings with it the potential for human and economic damage, each of them crosses borders indiscriminately, and each of them demands international cooperation in attacking and eradicating them.

The unilateralism and militarism of neoconservative national security strategies adopted by the Bush administration are wildly out of sync with today's global environment. The challenges we face today in managing a new geopolitical order and transnational threats can be dealt with only on a global, collaborative basis. Progressives need to put the country on a significantly different path of national security—one that is consistent with our values, focused on national needs, and based on empirical realities and genuine global threats. When viewed through the lens of sustainable security, the path to a stronger and safer America clearly requires that we make four major shifts in the direction of our global policy.

PHASED MILITARY REDEPLOYMENT FROM IRAQ

As my colleagues, Larry Korb and Brian Katulis, and I have argued in a number of CAP reports, the United States should immediately begin redeploying its troops from Iraq and declare it does not intend to maintain military bases permanently in Iraq.[5] A swift strategic redeployment from Iraq, coordinated with Iraq's government, gives the United States the best chance to revitalize ground forces now stretched too thin to address growing threats on other fronts in the fight against global terrorist groups in Afghanistan and elsewhere.

Getting troops out of the middle of Iraq's multiple conflicts while positioning troops in neighboring countries puts the United States in a better position to prevent Iraq's multiple sectarian conflicts from spreading beyond its borders, and gives Iraq and its neighbors the right incentive to help resolve Iraq's internal conflicts. It also would increase U.S. capacity to confront threats from global terrorist groups more effectively than our massive troop presence in Iraq currently does. U.S. armed forces need to regroup to fight the enemies we have, not referee Iraqi combatants with other scores to settle.

The United States should begin intense regional and international efforts to contain, manage, and ultimately resolve each of Iraq's conflicts. All of Iraq's neighbors have a stake in key aspects of Iraq's internal conflicts. The consequences of an escalated conflict in Iraq could be dire for these countries—more refugees, the possible spread of attacks by global terrorist groups such as al-Qaeda and its affiliates, and more crime and lawlessness. A sustained set of regional initiatives could help lessen the violence within Iraq and help reduce the potential threat of conflict spilling beyond Iraq's borders. These initiatives include enhancing border security, boosting cooperation on regional counterterrorism efforts, and encouraging security confidence-building measures to avoid more military conflict.

The United States also needs to pick up the pieces left by President Bush's broader failure in Middle East strategy by building a comprehensive sustained diplomatic approach across the region. We need to revive steady and regular diplomatic efforts to resolve the Arab-Israeli conflict, stabilize Lebanon, more effectively manage our interests in Syria, and address the threat posed by Iran. All of these challenges are interlinked, far more than when the United States invaded Iraq in 2003.

Repairing Our Military and Updating Its Mission

After five years of continuous war in Iraq, the U.S. military—despite the exceptional heroism of our servicemen and women—is barely able to contain the threats we face today, let alone the threats on the horizon. Our ground force is stretched to the breaking point by the war in Iraq, with attendant equipment shortages, manpower shortfalls, a misallocated budget, and training deficiencies.

As Army chief of staff Gen. George W. Casey Jr. described in testimony in 2008, "The cumulative effects of the last six-plus years at war have left our Army out of balance, consumed by the current fight and unable to do the things we know we need to do to properly sustain our all-volunteer force."[6] Already, every available Army combat brigade in the active-duty Army has served in Iraq or Afghanistan at least once, and many are now serving second and third tours. Thirty years' experience with the all-volunteer force shows that if the Army keeps soldiers away from home for more than one year out of three, retention rates will decline, especially among midcareer personnel such as Army captains, senior non-commissioned officers, and seasoned warrant officers, most of whom have not yet made a lifetime commitment to the Army.

The Army is doing everything it can to prevent the dam from breaking, but it is running out of fingers with which to plug the holes. In January 2005, after failing to hit its recruiting target, the Army raised the maximum enlistment age from thirty-five to forty. Six months later, after continuing to struggle, the Army raised its maximum age to forty-two. More alarming, recruitment standards are being lowered dramatically. The number of Army recruits who scored below average on its aptitude test doubled in 2006, and the Army has doubled the number of non-high school graduates it can enlist this year. With these lowered standards, the Government Accountability Office reported that cases of recruiter wrongdoing increased by 50 percent. Private Steven Green, who was arrested for his alleged role in the rape of an Iraqi girl and the murder of her family, received a waiver to enlist in the Army despite not having graduated from high school and having been arrested multiple times.

In addition to manpower shortages, the Army now has a $50 billion equipment shortage. In 2006, congressional Democrats revealed that a full two-thirds of the active U.S. Army is officially classified as "not ready for combat." The head of the National Guard responded to the news with a troubling announcement of his own: the National Guard is "in an even more dire situation than the active Army but both have the same symptoms; I just have a higher fever."[7]

In order to ensure that troops in Iraq have the equipment they need, the military has been sending equipment from non-deployed and reserve units, such as National Guard units in Louisiana and Mississippi. This means that it's extremely difficult for non-deployed units to train for combat; it also means that the Iraq War weakens even units not actually on the ground there.

The Marine Corps, America's emergency expeditionary force, also is under unprecedented strain. The unexpected use of the Corps as an occupying force in dangerous places such as Al-Anbar province caught the Marines off guard, and some units were deployed without basic equipment, such as body armor. A full year after the invasion of Iraq, many soldiers were compelled to buy their own body armor. According to a USA Today report, "Dan Britt paid about $1,400 for body armor for his son, a medic stationed in Kuwait who had orders to move into Baghdad."[8]

The unexpected role of the Marine Corps as a peacekeeping and occupying force undermines its ability to deploy rapidly and effectively across the globe—to be, as Marines proudly say, the "first to fight." Since 2003, the Marine Corps has maintained 40 percent of its ground equipment, 50 percent of its communications equipment, and 20 percent of its aviation assets in Iraq, where harsh conditions and combat losses are consuming resources at up to nine times its planned rate. To make up for the shortfalls, the Marines are raiding pre-positioned reserve equipment stocks in the Pacific and Europe. These equipment stocks include tanks and armored vehicles that have been positioned close to potential battlefields to allow immediate response. Some caches already have been depleted by 70 percent, seriously compromising the Marines' future rapid response capabilities.

The Marines are running out of helicopters, including the vital heavy-lift CH-53E Super Stallion. They are down to 150 CH-53Es, ten fewer than they require, and the situation will only worsen as they continue to lose these helicopters due to heavy use in Iraq. With replacement for these aging helicopters at least a decade off, this problem will hamper Marine readiness for years to come.

Compounding the problem, the Pentagon is on an unmatched spending spree, with an unaffordable eighty weapons systems— costing $1.6 *trillion*—in the pipeline, many designed for the types of conflicts the United States is unlikely to encounter again. The Pentagon's twenty-six largest acquisition programs are, on average, 40 percent above projected cost and 80 percent behind schedule. In the last four years, the projected cost of its five major weapons systems has risen by 85 percent.

The problem isn't the size of the regular Pentagon budget. During the past five and a half years, the regular defense budget, excluding the costs of the wars in Iraq and Afghanistan, has grown by more than $100 billion in inflation-adjusted dollars, to reach a post—World War II high. The problem is that the Defense Department has refused to make tough but necessary budget decisions. It allowed each of the services to maintain the same share of the budget as they did when Rumsfeld took the helm—despite the fact that the Army and the Marine Corps are bearing the brunt of the Iraq War. So when the Army budget rises, the Navy and Air Force budgets rise at the same rate, their chiefs fighting any efforts to cancel weapons programs, however misaligned with today's threats, to provide additional funding to the Army. In his nearly six years in office, as soldiers were sent to the desert without body armor or armor for their vehicles, Rumsfeld did away with only two major weapons programs, leaving untouched multibillion-dollar weapons programs whose mission was to counter the Soviet threat, such as the Air Force's F/A-22 fighter, the Navy's DDG 1000 destroyer, and the *Virginia*-class submarine.

All the while, our men and women in uniform suffer from neglect and misplaced priorities. As Melvin Laird, Richard Nixon's secretary of defense and the architect of the all-volunteer Army, explained, "People, not hardware, must be our highest priority." Even during the darkest days of the Cold War in the 1970s, when the Soviet military had sophisticated weaponry and many more troops than the United States, our military leaders repeatedly said that they would not trade our military for that of the Soviets because of the quality of our men and women in uniform.

The quality and dedication of our ground forces remain exceptional. But the pressures of sustained combat missions in Iraq and Afghanistan threaten to rupture the fragile confidence that is so critical to a healthy all-volunteer force. Operations in Iraq and Afghanistan reveal troubling cracks in the organization and structure of the more than one million U. S. ground forces—active, guard, and reserve. Overextension, overuse, and inattention to quality-of-life issues have become vulnerabilities. The pressures of asymmetric threats—lethal but less predictable than conventional tactics—will challenge our military leaders to recalibrate the approach to counterinsurgency, counterterrorism, post-conflict stabilization, and peacekeeping. In these complex environments, the quick response of our soldiers and Marines has more impact than expensive technology. Rethinking and developing plans and tactics—where language skills, neighborhood alliance, and economic development can deter conflict and save lives— becomes essential for giving our forces the right tools for success.

Dealing with Terrorism and Other Transnational Threats

As we recalibrate our global security strategy and repair the damage done to our soldiers and our great defense forces, we must come to grips with the fact that the overwhelming majority of the threats facing the country today do not have conventional military solutions. Military power will not erode the appeal of terrorism, roll back financial support for terrorists, secure fissile material in Russia or Pakistan, or win the war of ideas against the radical jihadists. Countering these threats instead requires the United States to marshal all the components of the country's national security arsenal.

In reality, a focus on prevention would decrease the need for conventional military force. Creating better intelligence and law enforcement capacities must be a first priority. We need to work with other nations to detect, disrupt, and destroy extremist networks bent on using terrorist force and violence. But we must also concentrate on promoting democracy, strengthening weak and failing states, alleviating poverty, and securing loose nuclear materials—all done in concert with our allies and multilateral institutions. These are far more effective at preventing problems than trying to bludgeon others into submission *after* situations have exploded out of control.

We should tackle our greatest challenges by acting according to our highest values. Transnational challenges breed in weak and failing states and are perpetuated by rogue regimes. Free and effective governments acting to improve the lives of their people and preserve the planet for future generations do not support terrorists or collapse into civil war. Stable, peaceful nations do not draw their neighbors into regional conflicts. While we cannot force democracy and peace on other nations or regions, we can nurture them with our actions and—at times—protect them with our presence.

Often, our most cynical actions—whether arming the Taliban in Afghanistan during the Soviet occupation, selling armaments to Saddam Hussein during the 1980s, or manufacturing evidence to justify a war—come back to haunt us. In contrast, from the Berlin airlift to American support for solidarity in Poland, the insertion of troops into Kosovo, and the Camp David accords, acting on our highest values as Americans has made the world better and our nation more secure.

As it was in the immediate aftermath of 9/11, the fight in Afghanistan is the perfect opportunity for U.S. leadership. Supported by the United Nations and NATO, we toppled the Taliban, disrupted al-Qaeda's base of operations, and helped place Afghanistan on a path toward functioning, democratic governance. But we diverted our attention and resources westwards, towards a misbegotten adventure in Iraq. We must reassert that leadership and resuscitate the international resolve to stabilize Afghanistan as increased Taliban activity threatens political gains in the nation.

To utilize our full arsenal of diplomatic and financial assets to bring about constructive change in the policies of our adversaries, we must be willing to talk to our enemies, as we did with the USSR, both bilaterally and through multilateral forums, because little is achieved through ostracism and veiled threats. It's hard to think of a more vivid example of this principle than our country's utter inability to influence events in Cuba. I have seen repression in Cuba, visited political dissidents, and have been forced to whisper questions over the sound of radios turned to blasting volumes so we could attempt to have conversations that wouldn't be overheard by government microphones. But after fifty years, it is time for engagement with the Cuban people and Cuban government, and time to get beyond a policy that is an artifact of the Cold War—a much more likely source of progress that will help this country's standing throughout Latin America and beyond. The current policy is self-defeating.

We also need to recognize that even peaceful nations must sometimes resort to force. Nations and non-state actors wishing to disrupt international peace and stability do exist, and there are clearly threats that can only be dealt with through force. The United States will never compromise its right and duty to use force to defend itself, fight terrorism, help safeguard international security, and prevent genocide and crimes against humanity.

For example, the United States needs to do more to act on the new doctrine of the "responsibility to protect" civilians whose governments cannot or will not afford them protection. For the longer term, this means enhancing our collective diplomatic, humanitarian, and military capabilities so that we can halt mass atrocities, in concert with the UN and allies. In real time, it means getting serious about Darfur, a crisis that both the White House and Congress have deemed genocide, but which after five years has been neither contained nor stopped. We should ramp up our diplomacy, ratchet up the pressure on Khartoum, and—given the regime's refusal to allow the full deployment of the hybrid UN/African Union peacekeeping force—work with NATO allies to develop alternative plans for civilian protection. If we listen to our collective conscience and act, we could save thousands, halt the spread of a regional war, and restore hope for a generation.

Strengthening international laws and institutions is a way to ensure that force will not have to be used—a lesson we know from the World War II and anti-communist successes forged by Franklin Roosevelt and Harry Truman. Similarly, unilateral action is risky and expensive. And, when force is necessary, multilateral military efforts are *less* costly and often *more* effective; the ability to build a fighting coalition is a good predictor of ultimate success. When the use of force cannot be avoided, the United States should strive to use it through international institutions, as we did in the Persian Gulf War, Kosovo, and our early successful efforts in Afghanistan.

We must remember that force helps to keep the peace as well as make war. Peacekeeping operations in Bosnia, Kosovo, East Timor, Haiti, Liberia, and elsewhere are testaments to the benefits of this approach. Finally, the United States must lead, forging effective laws and institutions that both deal with necessary threats and ease the burden on our nation and our troops, providing logistical support and strategic vision to multilateral military operations, bringing along allies, and clearly stating a moral and strategic case for intervention.

MODERNIZING INTERNATIONAL INSTITUTIONS AND ACCOMMODATING NEW POWERS

In today's shifting and fluid geopolitical environment, in which the United States must contend with challenges that range from peacefully managing the bold rise of China to rooting out clandestine terrorist cells to halting the spread of nuclear weapons, international institutions will play a decisive role. Actions such as Resolution 1373, by which nations agreed to halt transactions in arms and money to terrorist groups, would be nearly impossible without a mechanism such as the UN.[9]

But the UN is hampered by a Security Council whose membership reflects the post–World War II order, not that of the twenty-first century. The United States must lead a charge to reform the United Nations Security Council to include fast-growing powers from different regions and work to strengthen its support of the UN's humanitarian operations, such as the UN Development Programme (UNDP), the World Food Programme, and the Office of the UN High Commissioner for Refugees (UNHCR), all of which provide unique and invaluable services to the international community that individual nations cannot. In its response to the tsunami of 2004, the UN drew on the knowledge and expertise of many of its organizations to help relocate displaced people, provide food and supplies, offer medical help, and restore livelihoods. In addition, U.S. leadership on reform should be backed by our good standing, and a commitment to pay our arrears and pay our dues on time.

Similarly, repeated efforts to reform U.S. foreign aid have failed, leaving us with a broken system and without a single agency or individual in charge or responsible for the results. While President Bush has made commendable efforts to increase funding for global health, particularly to combat HIV/AIDS and malaria, other development needs have been neglected. It is time that we take bold action and elevate development to priority status by creating a new Department for International Development, headed by a cabinet-level secretary and charged with leading U.S. efforts to reduce poverty, build the capacity of states and societies to function as responsible members of the international community, and increase the opportunities available to those for whom violence is a more potent tool for change than is hope. By making development a priority, we can act on our values and strengthen the moral foundation from which to lead.

New American leadership in the international arena is also needed on the issue of energy and climate change. Energy and the effects of global warming are poised to be defining security issues in the next decade. We must reassert constructive U.S. leadership in the negotiations within the United Nations Framework Convention on Climate Change over a successor agreement to the Kyoto Protocol. And using the model of the G-8, the United States should help construct an effective E-8 of major economies to participate in an annual head-of-government meeting to hammer out concrete cooperative actions to invest in energy transformation and to reduce emissions.

Likewise, the international nonproliferation regime is in tatters and must be rebuilt. Though the use of force is often considered an option in the effort to stop regimes from acquiring nuclear weapons, an internationally coordinated set of carrots and sticks is the most effective way to reduce both the demand for nuclear weapons and the supply of materials, technology, and expertise needed to build them. On the demand side, the United States and global community must attack the root causes of proliferation and work to resolve the security conflicts that fuel proliferation—in the Middle East, South and East Asia, or wherever insecurities may lie. On the supply side, we must work with Russia, Pakistan, and other countries to ensure that the fissile materials needed to build bombs are secured against theft.

America must play a leadership role in ensuring that any further spread of peaceful nuclear technology is limited to energy reactors— and not the technologies needed to produce nuclear fuel. That will mean reinvigorating efforts to update the Nuclear Nonproliferation

Treaty and giving consideration to internationalizing the nuclear fuel cycle under the supervision of the International Atomic Energy Agency. We need to help developing nations acquire the governance capacity to prevent their territory from becoming a transit route or safe haven for the nuclear black market. Finally, we must get our own house in order by crafting a nuclear weapons posture that reflects the current threat environment, and not the threats of a bygone era. One of the first steps the United States can take is to eliminate unnecessary weapons in its nuclear stockpile and press other nuclear weapon states to follow suit.

Looking beyond near-term steps to restore America's security and standing in the world, we must also reflect on the long lessons of history and the consequences of taking unilateral actions rather than working in concert with international partners. In 1934, a moment in history placed squarely between the ruinous international effects of two world wars, Bertrand Russell noted the trends that had led to catastrophe in 1914 and were leading to it once again:

> The nineteenth century failed because it created no international organization. It inherited States from the past, and thought the problem solved when it made them into national States. In a haphazard way, as a result of technique unguided by thought, it created economic organizations which its philosophy did not teach it to control ... in spite of a great increase in wealth, intelligence, and happiness, the century which they attempted to guide ended in disaster.[10]

It took one more disaster, a few years later, to force the world to start getting it right. The creation of the United Nations, the Bretton Woods institutions, and NATO helped build a world where our ideals and philosophy finally caught up with the realities of power and politics. The United States played the leading role in the construction of this new, interconnected world, and achieved an unmatched prosperity and security.

America finds itself at a similar crossroads in its post-9/11 global affairs. We can either continue to stumble and employ outmoded concepts of security that have sparked regional and global crises, weakened our military, and left us isolated. Or, just as progressive leaders did following World War II, we can reclaim our historical role as a nation of great virtue and vision, willing to accept responsibility and abide by the rule of law and prepared to make the hard choices and sacrifices necessary to forge peace and prosperity. I am confident that this great country will choose its path wisely—a path paved long ago through the grand tradition of progressive internationalism.

Epilogue

On January 20, 2009, precisely at noon, the chief justice of the United States will administer the oath of office to America's forty-fourth president. It is possible that this new president will be a good and decent man, one who has a justly earned reputation for straight shooting and for his willingness to fight special interests to bring openness and honesty into the political process. He has taken a courageous stand on the contentious subject of immigration, and his commitment to fighting climate change is perhaps the most determined that his party offers.

Nonetheless, John McCain's election would be a catastrophe for the United States. He has sworn to follow the current administration's failed path into the Iraqi desert, regardless of the destruction and dishonor found along that way. Rather than mopping up the fiscal mess created by tax cuts designed to make the affluent even richer, he has doubled down, proposing to increase our national debt with a further $2 trillion or more in tax cuts, more than half of which would find their way into the pockets of America's richest 1 percent. He is eager to privatize a health care system that already fails one American in six. And under pressure from his own party, he renounced his own immigration reform bill. Four years of John McCain will be four more years of the conservative government that has led this country to the brink of disaster.

But I am an optimist, despite the battles of the last eight years. I believe that our next presidency will be a historic one, not only because the person taking the oath that Tuesday morning, exactly ten weeks after Election Day, will be the first American of color to be sworn in, but also because the four years that follow that day will bring a transformation of the way we live and a restoration of America's leadership role in the world. Barack Obama understands the urgency of breaking sharply and immediately with the Bush administration's conservative path; he understands the extraordinary challenges we must face right now, and the importance of harnessing the power of our best progressive traditions to transform the way we deal with our climate, economy, and security.

There can be no half measures if we are to protect Americans' way of life and the opportunity to work and succeed that my family enjoyed and that put me where I am today. In 1993, my wife and I stood on the west front of the Capitol, with the leadership of the Congress and the leadership of Bill Clinton's new government and watched him take the oath of office. It was an extraordinary moment for the grandson and granddaughter of penniless immigrants. I believe that Inauguration Day 2009 will be an extraordinary day as well for millions of Americans who yearn for the same opportunity to succeed that I had, and for billions around the world who yearn for the kind of global leadership that the United States once showed, built on justice and compassion as well as determination and strength.

What follows, is what I hope that they, and I, will hear.

Forty-fourth President of the United States of America

Inaugural Remarks

Washington, D.C.

January 20, 2009

Today, the American people are summoned to save our country and to heal our world at a time when all that we hold precious is at stake. Meeting these challenges will take all of us, working together as a united people in an interdependent world, as never before. But if we live by the words of our Creator, who taught us to thirst for righteousness, to show mercy, and to make peace, if we as citizens honor the example of our Founders, we can surmount these challenges and make this a prosperous and more peaceful century for us and for the world.

Think of what America has already done. A breakaway, rebellious republic became a global leader. A society that once exploited slave labor is now enriched by its diversity. A wilderness gave birth to the world's largest, strongest economy. A nation comfortable in its continental isolation became an international force for democracy, freedom, and the common good. No tyrant, no disease, no depression, no challenge has ever been a match for the common decency and uncommon goodness of the people we call our fellow citizens.

Yet today we are challenged as never before.

Standing together, we must find the resources and the inner strength to manage three extraordinary transformations at the very same moment.

We must change the way we produce and consume energy, in order to save the planet from climate change and the environmental security and economic crises global warming will bring.

We must reinvigorate our economy and integrate it into the

global market in ways that make our products more competitive, our families more secure, and our system more just.

And we must build a new security structure, joining with our allies to oppose rogue nations and terrorist cells, while winning the smaller battles for hearts and minds with humanitarian aid, with trade, and with the public expression of our greatest ideals.

Three great challenges for one great nation; each of them affecting one another, meaning none of them can be solved alone. There is no security while we rely on the foreign oil that funds our enemies, heats our climate, threatens whole populations, and constricts our economy; there is no prosperity when job growth is weak, health care is at risk, and families are losing their homes; and there can be no answer to global warming until we reinvent our economy and create new jobs at home employing Americans in ways that cleanse the earth's air of greenhouse gas pollution.

These are the interlocking challenges that must be at the heart of America's project in the years and decades that lie ahead. If we resolve them—and it will take extraordinary and united efforts to do so—we will open the doors to a new era of prosperity and security, and make us worthy in the eyes of our children as we pass a better country on to them.

These are not tasks that America can undertake alone. But this is a struggle which the world looks to us to lead, which we are uniquely qualified to do. We come to this crossroads thanks to a distinctly American genius that has grown larger and more creative with each ensuing generation.

We arrived at this place because we have had from our earliest days a government truly of the people. We have not always been perfect or just. But when this government has been strong and bold, it has made people's lives better. Again and again—from roads and railroads to outer space and the Internet, from the Homestead

Act to the right to own a home, the right to attend college, and yes, the right to form a union and fight for better wages and safer work—the government created opportunity, and the American people in turn created an engine of economic growth at home and a force for liberty and democracy around the world.

Not far from here there is a statue of Franklin Roosevelt sitting in his wheelchair, the president who helped us banish fear from American life, who led a determined world against tyranny and evil, who put America back on its feet when depression and hopelessness laid us low. But to me, the bronze and granite of that monument speak even more eloquently of the men and women who answered his call to save our country and then to save our world.

Today we face challenges as great as those they overcame, yet our capacity to meet these challenges has been diminished for too long by neglect of our people at home and neglect of our partners across the globe. To unite the world, we must join it as Roosevelt's generation did, in a grand alliance, dedicated to the ideas and strategies that will forever transform the way we live, work, and interact with one another: creating opportunity at home and on a global scale, not just for the rich but for the poor and the middle class; embracing the coalitions that kept the world safe during the Cold War while creating new structures for international cooperation; trusting millions of Americans to embrace the challenge, share the sacrifice, and work together for the common good; and holding on to a faith that carries us through times of trial and reminds us that we labor not just for ourselves and this moment, but for our fellow citizens of the earth God gave us, and for those who will live in it after our time.

For too long, as the world changed, some of our leaders tried to tell us that we didn't have to. While some said America could remain affluent and self-reliant without accounting for a changing world, the changing world proved them wrong.

Four hundred years ago, it was hard for many to accept that the universe did not revolve around the earth, that Copernicus and Galileo were right in their assessment of our position in the heavens. But the truth did not harm us. Our understanding of science did not threaten our faith; our new knowledge became the springboard for brilliant leaps in physics and astronomy, and made our lives better. Just the same, our understanding that our earth does not revolve around our nation—that we can still lead, but that we must do so by consensus, by example, by the force of our ideas and our willingness to compromise—will not lessen our greatness as a people. Rather, it will give us the understanding that we need to join our allies in leading history down a new path, one of progress and understanding.

And we will walk that path together, as one family, one community, one nation.

To begin, we will transform America's approach to energy and the environment, so that we can join the effort to heal this earth from the scourge of global warming, and power our economy with fuels and technology that protect not just the climate but also our national security and our standard of living.

We make no apologies for our affluence, but we fool no one but ourselves if we think we can consume a quarter of this world's fossil fuels without fouling the air, arming our enemies, and competing for resources with billions of families whose aspirations for wealth and opportunity are no different from our own.

In this effort, as in all of our undertakings, our government must keep a delicate balance. To one side lies a government that burdens rather than unites, and leads not to solutions but to bureaucracy and confusion. To the other lies an indifference to the common good and a veneration of material wealth that brings corruption, exploitation, and the abuse of a great nation and its people by powerful elites.

Government can set the course. But we understand that individual initiative, the empowerment of our people through education, ingenuity, and economic incentive will power our voyage. We succeed by being united in common purpose, with bold public leadership, scientific innovation, and an energized private economy.

Government can regulate as well, but our economy will grow faster and better if a new embrace of corporate ethics comes not from regulators' heavy hands but from businesspeople's change of hearts. Openness and honesty must extend beyond campaigns and governing to small businesses and multinational enterprise. Let us become an economy of rapid innovation, honest accounting, and respect for employees and shareholders, rather than one marked by paper profits and outright fraud.

So I call today for America to embrace an audacious target: that 25 percent of our nation's fuels be derived from alternative energy sources—such as wind, bioenergy, and the sun. And I call for the adoption of a cap-and-trade system that will force producers of greenhouse gasses to live within a cap on pollution that will decline by 80 percent by midcentury.

These are extraordinary goals. But meeting them will bring extraordinary gains. An auto industry that leads in green technology could revitalize factory towns throughout the Midwest. Wind power, solar power, and bioenergy derived from sources such as switchgrass and farm and municipal wastes will bring jobs and wealth to rural areas that have been bypassed in a global economy. New technology that captures and stores the CO_2 pollution from our coal-fired electrical plants will mean jobs in coalfields and in factories sending new technologies around the world.

Energy transformation is not only an ecological imperative. Our economic policy must be rooted in a comprehensive effort to slow and reverse global warming—one of the great challenges in the history of humanity. I am a great believer in the power of America's private sector and its partners and competitors to find solutions. But history teaches us that breakthroughs come from collaboration between government and industry. That's how we reached the moon. That's how we built the Internet. And that's how we cut our cars' emissions by 90 percent and rapidly reduced the sources of acid rain faster and more cheaply than even the most optimistic among us imagined.

Although America's private sector will always be the first engine of true economic recovery, our government must lead by example, by getting our house in order, freeing capital now consumed by the federal government for America's private firms, and financing the investments in people and infrastructure that will ensure sustained and broad-based economic growth.

The tax and budget policies of the last eight years have opened an unacceptable chasm in our society at a deepening cost to working families, forcing the United States to borrow trillions of dollars from governments overseas to pay for oil bought overseas.

Our national debt stands at $9 trillion; our profligacy means that our government doesn't have enough funds for roads and bridges, education and training, health care and R&D. We will change that, with tax reform that is fair, simple, pro-growth, and pro-work. Most Americans will enjoy an increase in their take-home pay. A handful of America's richest families will pay a little more. But all Americans will enjoy an economy that is growing faster and producing better jobs and a work force that is better supported and prepared.

Increased revenue will lower the deficit and finance a greater contribution to educating our children at every level. We make this effort central to economic recovery, because we will depend on children ready to learn, on young adults and workers starting out leaving school having learned as much as their competitors abroad. Support for higher education will be coupled with lifelong learning opportunities so that every individual who studies and works hard has a chance to achieve and hold middle-class status today. If our efforts to resolve climate change and oil dependence are to be anchored to our economic goals, we must have skilled engineers, talented technicians, and trained workers in factories and laboratories, building a green economy for the twenty-first century.

Even workers who do not go on to become scientists or investment bankers should have an opportunity to enjoy the fruits of our nation's great wealth. We will work with Congress to make the minimum wage a living wage, increased significantly and pegged to inflation for workers' protection. We will restore federal protections for workers who want to join a union. And we will increase the Earned Income Tax Credit, expand the child tax credit, and provide child care support for poor working families with young children. As President Bill Clinton said so well, no child with a parent working full-time should be forced to grow up in poverty. Our goal will be to cut poverty in half in the next ten years.

Nothing is more critical to the health of our economy than a health care system that covers every American. Under our plan, most Americans will continue to get their coverage as they do now, through their workplace. But the forty-seven million Americans who aren't covered today will have options they've never enjoyed before. Some federal programs will be expanded, such as SCHIP and Medicaid, to cover the very poorest working families. For the rest, we'll make private coverage more affordable with tax credits to help defray costs and a new pool that lets individuals and small businesses get coverage at the same rates large employers enjoy. We'll rely on the best parts of our private system to resolve America's greatest public health care crisis.

And as we shore up the earning power of American workers, we should look to workers on other shores as well. The problems and the benefits of trade are global now: the ability to exploit workers in Saipan can easily mean jobs lost in South Carolina. Improving living standards and environmental protection across the world is not only just, it creates new and growing markets for our own products, and makes it less likely our jobs will be sent offshore. Americans respect the desire of people in every nation to enjoy the living standards we enjoy. The idea that every person should have decent work that enriches rather than exploits and provides the means for advancement and security is an American ideal that, like democracy and peace, we should seek to extend to every nation.

Finally, we must protect our prosperity and our lives by joining with other nations to create a new kind of security, one rooted in respect for America as a moral leader as well as a military power. America will continue to hunt down terrorists. But the grief Americans knew on 9/11 is shared by those who have lost loved ones in Bali and Madrid and London and other sites of brutal actions around the world. Our intelligence and police work must be shared as well. And so must the understanding that we will win this war not just by jailing people but also by educating and elevating them.

Our security strategy begins with a drawdown of American troops in Iraq, a new focus on the resurgent Taliban in neighboring Afghanistan, and a return of as many of our exhausted troops to their homes and their families as possible. These brave men and women have done everything asked of them, and more, for six long years of war. As American warriors have proved from the first hours of our republic, our men and women under arms are second to none in the courage and intelligence needed to keep our country safe. I salute them and I thank them.

But their commander in chief recognizes that our troops cannot and should not carry the burden of America's security so fully on their shoulders alone. That burden should be shared by intelligence agencies and police operation, by close allies, and sometimes by unsavory competitors with whom we share common security goals. It should be shared by diplomats and health officials, and by multilateral institutions designed not to fight wars but to prevent them.

We should tackle our greatest challenges by acting according to our highest values. Free and effective governments in nations who receive respect and enjoy the potential for economic progress rarely breed terrorists or collapse into civil war. Stable or peaceful nations do not draw their neighbors into regional conflicts. While we cannot force democracy and peace on other nations or regions, we can nurture them with our actions and—at times—protect them with our presence.

Indeed, it is vital that we work closely both to win wars and to prevent them through international institutions like the United Nations. Drought relief, food distributions, refugee care, and peace-keeping missions led by international organizations and supported by the U.S. are not only the right thing to do, they are the smart thing to do. And we will continue the program begun by President Bush which has done so much to ease suffering and save lives in the developing world, by assisting victims of HIV-AIDS, tuberculosis, and malaria in the developing world, and working to slow their deadly spread.

Four years ago we saw how effective the UN and other multilateral institutions could be, when they brought aid to millions of victims of the Indian Ocean tsunami. Our contribution to this global effort saved lives and sped the recovery. It also proved to millions of people, mainly Muslim, that Americans are a people whose compassion extends to those of every background. We made the world better, and safer.

History does not stand still, and history is littered with king-doms and empires and nations who hid from change behind intel-lectual Maginot Lines—so effective at fighting the last war, so useless in an era of change. Today, we face challenges that were barely acknowledged a generation ago, that could devastate us by the time the next generation comes of age.

When I was young, I loved reading American history, the sto-ries and the struggles, the heroes in battle and the great leaders of our world. But it wasn't until I was older that I realized what was truly important about our nation's story. It wasn't that we were per-fect, because we weren't. It wasn't the exact date that Washington crossed the Delaware, although I can tell you that. It wasn't even to avoid the mistakes that others have made, because history never repeats itself exactly.

The most important thing that I learned from American his-tory is the power of progress—that we have a capacity for greatness that we summon when we recognize a challenge, when progress is needed in the ways of the world. A greatness that comes less from our leaders than from our people: from farmers whose ploughs tamed the wilderness; from immigrants who came with nothing but whose hard work built the greatest factories on the planet and whose unions created the middle class; from office clerks who sailed for France to save the world; from seamstresses who refused to sit in the back of the bus. The lesson I learned is that in times of crisis, the American people can be counted on to lead and to change the world.

As I think of the magnitude of the battles ahead, I think not just of challenge but of the opportunity for Americans to show again the greatness that resides within all of us and our nation. The fight for our climate, our economy, and our lives will not be won by me or by a handful of cabinet officials or corporate leaders. Already I can al-most feel the energy and the enthusiasm the youth of this nation will bring to this call for public service, their eagerness to leave their mark on a changing world, and their understanding of the stake their generation has in our success. And I know that they will be joined by millions of others of us, older perhaps but yet unwearied, ready to work hard, share sacrifices, and devote ourselves to uncounted acts of small genius and strong determination that together accrue into greatness—with the eyes and the judgment of the world upon us all.

We are asked to soar. When I look to the history of this great nation and think of all whom I have met in my years in public life, I believe with all of my heart that we can do so.

NOTES

LIGHTNING ROUND
(20 SECONDS TO ANSWER):
WHAT DOES IT MEAN TO BE A PROGRESSIVE?

1. See Eldon J. Eisenach, *The Social and Political Thought of American Progressivism*, Hackett Publishing Company, 2006; and John Recchiuti, *Civic Engagement: Social Science and Progressive-Era Reform in New York City*, University of Pennsylvania Press, 2007.

2. The election of 1912 is frequently cited as a clear demarcation between these two ideas, with Woodrow Wilson's New Freedom capturing the original Jeffersonian argument, as expressed by Louis Brandeis, and Teddy Roosevelt's New Nationalism, as expressed by Herbert Croly, proffering the defense of expanded executive authority and national powers to meet the rise of concentrated capitalism and make the most of it. Although most historians believe the differences between these approaches were minimal in terms of real governing, the theoretical divergences are instructive.

3. Eric Goldman, *Rendezvous with Destiny: A History of Modern American Reform*, Vintage Books, 1956, p. 55.

4. William Graham Sumner, *What Social Classes Owe to Each Other*, 1883.

CHAPTER 1
LESSON ONE:
PROGRESSIVES STAND WITH PEOPLE, NOT PRIVILEGE

1. Henry George, *Progress and Poverty*, Cosimo Classics, 2005, p. 9.

2. For more on Henry George's influence on progressives, see: Daniel Aron, *Men of Good Hope*, Oxford University Press, 1951; Henry Steele Commager, *The American Mind*, Yale University Press, 1950; Ray Ginger, *The Nationalizing of American Life, 1877–1900*, Free Press, 1965; Eric Goldman, *Rendezvous with Destiny: A History of Modern American Reform*, Vintage Books, 1956, p. 55; George Mowry, *The Era of Theodore Roosevelt and the Birth of Modern America, 1900–1912*, Harper Torchbooks, 1958; and Robert Wiebe, *The Search for Order, 1877–1920*, Hill and Wang, 1967. For more on George's influence in Britain, see Alan Grimes's introduction to L. T. Hobhouse, *Liberalism*, Oxford University Press, 1964.

3. John Kenneth Galbraith, *The Affluent Society*, Houghton Mifflin, 1997, p. 44.

4. Robert Wiebe, *The Search for Order, 1877–1920*, Hill and Wang, 1967, p. 137.

5. Eric Goldman, pp. 24–25.

6. Robert Wiebe, p. 79.

7. James Chace, *1912: Wilson, Roosevelt, Taft and Debs—The Election That Changed the Country*, Simon and Schuster, 2004, pp. 80–81.

8. People's Party Platform, *Omaha Morning World-Herald*, July 5, 1892.

9. As quoted in Richard Hofstadter, *The Age of Reform*, Vintage Books, 1955, p. 64.

10. Jack Beatty, *Age of Betrayal: The Triumph of Money in America, 1865–1900*, Knopf, 2007, p. 332.

11. Eric Goldman, p. 41.

12. Richard Hofstadter, p. 78.

13. Jack Beatty, pp. 330–32. The biracialism of the Populist movement is contested among historians. Some, such as C. Vann Woodward, believed there was a genuine uniting of class interests among the poor across racial lines, even in the South, to challenge economic power and oppression. Others dispute this notion, citing differences between their rhetoric of support for blacks and their actions in office. Beatty ultimately agrees with James Clarke that, "[a]ll in all, the Populist record in the region is not what its proponents claim it to be, but neither should it be read with complete contempt."

14. Michael Kazin, *A Godly Hero: The Life of William Jennings Bryan*, Knopf, 2006, xiv.

15. Like the single tax, the mantra of "free silver" reflects the early progressive desire to find some dramatic way to break with the status quo and help out the working class. Many agrarian progressives and Bryan supporters believed that minting more silver money along with gold-backed currency would allow severely indebted farmers and homeowners to get out from under their oppression. Wage earners and more urban reformers were skeptical of silver as an answer, due to the inflationary effects on jobs and wages, and never fully supported the effort.

16. Michael Kazin, p. 65.

17. Walter Rauschenbusch, *Christianity and the Social Crisis*, HarperCollins, 2007, p. xxi and p. 31.

18. Ibid., p. 229.

19. Jean Bethke Elshtain, *Jane Addams and the Dream of American Democracy*, Basic Books, 2002, p. 96.

20. Ibid., p. 100.

21. See United States Conference of Catholic Bishops, *Compendium of the Social Doctrine of the Church*, USCCB Publishing, 2003, p. 39.

22. Jean Bethke Elshtain, p. 60.

23. James Chace, pp. 186–87.

CHAPTER 2
LESSON TWO:
PROGRESSIVES BELIEVE IN THE COMMON GOOD,
AND A GOVERNMENT THAT OFFERS A HAND UP

1. George Mowry, *Theodore Roosevelt and the Birth of Modern America, 1900–1912*, Harper Torchbooks, 1958, p. 87.

2. Theodore Roosevelt, "New Nationalism," Osawatomie, Kansas, 1910. See http://www.teachingamericanhistory.org/library/index.asp?document=501.

3. See David Von Drehle, *Triangle: The Fire That Changed America*, Grove Press, 2004.

4. Henry F. Pringle, *Theodore Roosevelt*, Harvest Books, 1931, p. 300.

5. Lincoln Steffens, "Tweed Days in St. Louis," *McClure's Magazine*, 1902.

6. Justin Kaplan, *Lincoln Steffens*, Simon and Schuster, 2004, p. 118.

7. Lincoln Steffens, *Autobiography of Lincoln Steffens*, Harcourt, Brace, 1931, p. 474.

8. George Mowry, pp. 62–63.

9. David P. Thelen, *Robert M. La Follette and the Insurgent Spirit*, Little, Brown, 1976.

10. "A Third of a Century of La Folletteism: Being a Survey of the Origin, Development, Struggles, and Accomplishments of the Progressives in Wisconsin Politics," *Milwaukee Journal*, October 21, 1930.

11. Robert Marion La Follette, *Autobiography*, La Follette's: A Personal Narrative of Political Experiences, Robert M. LaFollette Co., 1913, p. x.

12. Henry Steele Commager, *The American Mind*, Yale University Press, 1950, p. 352.

13. Theodore Roosevelt, "A Charter for Democracy," speech delivered to Ohio State Constitutional Convention, February 21, 1912. http://www.teachingamericanhistory.org/library/index.asp?document=1126.

14. Alice Honeywell, *La Follette and His Legacy*, University of Wisconsin Madison, Office of University Publications, 1984.

15. Robert Marion La Follette, p. 344.

16. Ibid., p. 346.

17. George Mowry, p. 74.

18. Benjamin Gue, *History of Iowa from the Earliest Times to the Beginning of the Twentieth Century*, Century History, 1903, pp. 209–10.

19. Henry Pringle, p. 300.

20. Tweed Roosevelt, "Theodore Roosevelt: A Brief Biography," Theodore Roosevelt Association, 2003.

21. Theodore Roosevelt, "Address to the National Conference of the Governors of the United States," May 13-15, 1908.

22. George Mowry, p. 214.

23. Edmund Morris, *Theodore Rex*, Random House, 2001, pp. 517–19.

24. Michael McGerr, foreword to Herbert Croly, *The Promise of American Life*, Northeast University Press, p. xii.

25. Arthur Link, *Woodrow Wilson and the Progressive Era, 1910–1917*, Harper Collins, 1954, p. 14.

26. Ibid., p. 16.

27. Theodore Roosevelt, "Confession of Faith," Address to the Progressive Party convention, 1912.

28. Arthur Link, pp. 20–21.

29. As quoted in ibid., p. 79.

30. Michael McGerr, *A Fierce Discontent: The Rise and Fall of the Progressive Movement in America, 1870–1920*, Oxford University Press, 2005, p. 281.

31. Geoffrey Stone, *Perilous Times: Free Speech in Wartime from the Sedition Act of 1798 to the War on Terrorism*, Norton, 2004, pp. 172–3.

32. Alan Brinkley, "Past As Prologue?" in *Liberty Under Attack: Reclaiming Our Freedoms in an Age of Terror*, edited by Richard C. Leone and Greg Anrig, Jr., Public Affairs, 2007, p. 33.

33. Paul Starr, *Freedom's Power*, Basic Books, 2007, p. 111. See L. T. Hobhouse, *Liberalism*, for the British description.

34. Paul Starr, p. 315.

35. Harold Faulkner, *American Political and Social History*, F. S. Crofts, 1945, pp. 688–89.

36. Franklin Roosevelt, *Looking Forward*, John Day, 1933, p. 17.

37. Arthur Schlesinger Jr., *The Coming of the New Deal*, Mariner Books, 2003, p. 18.

38. Ibid., pp. 13, 35.

39. Harold Faulkner, p. 689.

40. Arthur Schlesinger Jr., pp. 20–21.

41. Jonathan Alter, *The Defining Moment: FDR's Hundred Days and the Triumph of Hope*, Simon and Schuster, 2006, p. 329.

42. Ibid., p. 332.

CHAPTER 3
LESSON THREE:
PROGRESSIVES HOLD THAT ALL PEOPLE
ARE EQUAL IN THE EYES OF GOD AND UNDER THE LAW

1. Paul Starr, *Freedom's Power*, Basic Books, 2007, p. 163.

2. George Mowry, *Theodore Roosevelt and the Birth of Modern America, 1900–1912*, Harper Torchbooks, 1958, p. 94.

3. Jean Bethke Elshtain, *Jane Addams and the Dream of American Democracy*, Basic Books, 2002, p. 200.

4. Elizabeth Cady Stanton, *A History of Woman Suffrage*, vol. 1., Fowler and Sons, 1881, pp. 70–71.

5. Ellen Carol DuBois, in *A Companion to American Thought*, edited by Richard Fox and James Kloppenberg, Blackwell, 1998, p. 652.

6. Eric Goldman, *Rendezvous with Destiny: A History of Modern American Reform*, Vintage Books, 1958, p. 137.

7. W. E. B. Du Bois, *The Souls of Black Folk*, A. C. McClurgand Co., 1903.

8. Quotes from "Address to the Country," from the second Niagara Movement conference in Harpers Ferry, WVA, 1906. See http://www.math.buffalo.edu/~sww/ohistory/hwny-niagara-movement.html.

9. From "History of the NAACP," http://www.naacp.org/about/history/timeline/index.htm.

10. Eleanor Roosevelt, "Race, Religion and Prejudice," *New Republic* 106, May 11, 1942.

11. See http://www.ardemgaz.com/prev/central/prestext26.html.

12. For a good overview of King's intellectual framework, see Stephen Oates, *Let the Trumpet Sound: A Life of Martin Luther King, Jr.*, HarperPerennial, 1994.

13. David Chappell, *A Stone of Hope: Prophetic Religion and the Death of Jim Crow*, University of North Carolina Press, 2004, p. 54.

14. Stephen Oates, pp. 70–71.

15. As recounted by Yancey Martin in Howell Raines, *My Soul Is Rested: The Story of the Civil Rights Movement in the Deep South*, Penguin Classics, 1983, p. 61.

16. Howell Raines, p. 69.

17. David Chappell, p. 87.

18. Martin Luther King Jr., "A Letter from Birmingham Jail." See http://www.stanford.edu/group/King/frequentdocs/birmingham.pdf.

19. David J. Garrow, *Bearing the Cross: Martin Luther King, Jr., and the Southern Christian Leadership Conference*, Perennial Classics, 1999, pp. 258–59.

20. James Ralph Jr., "Home Truths: Dr. King and the Chicago Freedom Move-ment," *American Visions*, August–September, 1994, http://findarticles.com/p/articles/mi_m1546/is_n4_v9/ai_15752030.

21. Today's conservatives are still trying to explain away how Reagan ended up so close to this tragic site and how he was not sending a signal about states' rights, in much the same way that Pat Buchanan was forced to explain the use of the Nazi cemetery at Bitburg for a White House photo op.

22. Barack Obama, "A More Perfect Union," speech delivered in Philadelphia, Pennsylvania, March 2008. See http://my.barackobama.com/page/content/hisownwords/.

CHAPTER 4
LESSON FOUR:
PROGRESSIVES STAND FOR UNIVERSAL HUMAN
RIGHTS AND COOPERATIVE GLOBAL SECURITY

1. For an extended analysis of this position see Michael Lind, *The American Way of Strategy: U.S. Foreign Policy and the American Way*, Oxford University Press, 2006.

2. Kevin Mattson, *When America Was Great: The Fighting Faith of Postwar Liberalism*, Routledge, 2006, pp. 176–77.

3. From the records of the Anti-Imperialist League, Swarthmore College.

4. Platform of the Anti-Imperialist League, 1899.

5. Michael Kazin, *A Godly Hero: The Life of William Jennings Bryan*, Knopf, 2006, p. 103.

6. Ibid., p. 233.

7. Jean Bethke Elshtain, *Jane Addams and the Dream of American Democracy*, Basic Books, 2002, p. 206.

8. Richard Wightman Fox and James T. Kloppenberg, eds., *A Companion to American Thought*, Blackwell, 1998, p. 15.

9. Eric Goldman, *Rendezvous with Destiny: A History of Modern American Reform*, Vintage Books, 1956, pp. 184–85.

10. Walter Lippman, "The End of American Isolation," *The New Republic*, November 7, 1914.

11. Woodrow Wilson's, "War Message" before Congress, April 2, 1917. See http://www.firstworldwar.com/source/usawardeclaration.htm.

12. Harold Faulkner, *American Political and Social History*, F. S. Crofts, 1945, p. 615.

13. Ibid., pp. 623–24.

14. Herbert Croly, "Liberalism vs. War," *New Republic*, December 8, 1920.

15. Eric Goldman, p. 207.

16. Harold Faulkner, p. 625.

17. http://chicora.org/woodrow_wilson.htm.

18. For more see Alan Brinkley, "A Familiar Story: Lessons from Past Assaults on Freedoms," in *The War on Our Freedoms: Civil Liberties in an Age of Terrorism*, edited by Richard C. Leane and Greg Anria Jr., Public Affairs, 2003.

19. Richard Wightman Fox and James T. Kloppenberg, p. 751.

20. Harold Faulkner, pp. 741–43.

21. Ibid., p. 743.

22. Article 1, United Nations Declaration of Human Rights, adopted and proclaimed by General Assembly resolution 217 A (III) of December 10, 1948.

23. Eleanor Roosevelt, "Address to the General Assembly of the United Nations," December 9, 1948.

24. Douglas Brinkley, *The Unfinished Presidency: Jimmy Carter's Journey Beyond the White House*, Penguin Books, 1999, p. 211.

25. Arthur Schlesinger Jr., *The Vital Center*, Riverside Press, 1962, p. 223.

26. Ibid., chapter 3.

27. Kevin Mattson, p. 178.

28. Some people conflate the lessons of Nixon's 1972 triumph with those of his victory over Hubert Humphrey in 1968. The lesson of 1972 is that if you allow your opponent to portray you as weak, national security centrists will desert your candidacy in droves. The lesson of the 1968 campaign is perhaps simpler: if you have a riot at your convention, your party is unlikely to come together behind you in time for the fall campaign.

CHAPTER 5
BILL CLINTON:
A MODERN PROGRESSIVE

1. Alan White, "Reagan's AIDS Legacy Silence Equals Death," *San Francisco Chronicle*, June 8, 2004.

2. President William J. Clinton, "Economic Address to a Joint Session of Congress," February 18, 1993. See http://query.nytimes.com/gst/fullpage.html?res= 9F0CEEDB1F3CF93BA25751C0A965958260.

3. http://research.stlouisfed.org/fred2/data/UNRATE.txt.

4. U.S. Department of Labor, Bureau of Labor Statistics, http://www.gpoaccess .gov/usbudget/fy02/erp.html, Table b-42.

5. Congressional Budget Office Analysis, "The State Children's Health Insurance Program," May 2007, http://www.cbo.gov/doc.cfm?index=8092&type=0& sequence=1.

6. U.S. Bureau of the Census, Current Population Survey, Annual Social and Economic Supplements, http://www.wnjpin.state.nj.us/OneStopCareerCenter/LaborMarketInformation/lmi19/HI-4.htm.

7. Ibid.

8. Kaiser Family Foundation Employer Health Benefit Survey 2007, Summary of Findings, Exhibit 1, http://www.kff.org/insurance/loader.cfm?url=/commonspot/security/getfile.cfm&PageID=13525.

9. Kaiser Family Foundation Employer Health Benefit Survey 2007, Summary of Findings, Exhibit B, http://www.kff.org/insurance/7672/upload/Summary-of-Findings-EHBS-2007.pdf.

10. Ibid.

11. A. G. Kenwood and A. L. Lougheed, *The Growth of the International Economy 1820–2000*, 4th edition, Routledge, 1999, p. 294.

12. http://clinton4.nara.gov/WH/Accomplishments/additional.html (Education Department, April 2, 1999; Treasury Department, FY 2001 budget, p. 49).

Chapter 6
George W. Bush:
A Disastrous Conservative

1. http://www.cbo.gov/ftpdocs/90xx/doc9074/04-18-StandBudget.pdf.

2. http://blog.washingtonpost.com/the-trail/2008/03/21/the_new_hyde_park_project.html.

3. http://pewglobal.org/reports/display.php?ReportID=252.

4. William Saletan, "Deathbed Conversion," http://www.slate.com/id/2115879.

5. Think Progress timeline on Katrina, http://thinkprogress.org/katrina-timeline.

Chapter 7
Solving the Global Warming Crisis

1. For more see http://www.americanprogress.org/issues/2007/11/pdf/energy_chapter.pdf.

2. http://www.washingtonpost.com/wp-dyn/content/article/2006/10/30/AR2006103000269.html.

3. http://www.sciencemag.org/cgi/content/full/306/5702/1686.

4. http://www.americanprogress.org/issues/2008/01/capandtrade101.html.

5. "Record U.S. hybrid sales expected," Associated Press, August 2, 2007, available at http://www.wheels.ca/article/30377.

6. David Sandalow, *Freedom From Oil: How the Next President Can End the United States' Oil Addiction,* McGraw-Hill, 2007.

7. http://www.ethanolrfa.org/media/press/rfa/view.php?id=964.

8. http://www.bls.gov/news.release/cpi.nr0.htm.

9. Jake Caldwell, "Fueling a New Farm Economy: Creating Incentives for Biofuels in Agriculture and Trade Policy," Center for American Progress, 2007.

10. Reid Ewing et al., "Growing Cooler: The Evidence on Urban Development and Climate Change," Urban Land Institute, 2007. See http://www.smartgrowth america.org/gcindex.html.

11. Ibid.

12. http://www.eia.doe.gov/oiaf/1605/flash/flash.html.

13. http://web.mit.edu/coal/.

14. Union of Concerned Scientists, "Renewing America's Economy," http://www.ucsusa.org/clean_energy/renewable_energy_basics/renewing-americas-economy.html.

15. "The Investment Pays Off" Report by the Assistant Secretary for Fossil Energy U.S. DOE November 1999 http://www.gao.gov/new.items/d01854t.pdf.

CHAPTER 8
RESTORING THE AMERICAN DREAM
IN A GLOBAL ECONOMY

1. Robert M. Solow, "A Contribution to the Theory of Economic Growth," *Quarterly Journal of Economics* 70 (1956).

2. http://media.www.dailytrojan.com/media/storage/paper679/news/2005/09/30/News/U.s-Falls.In.Education.Rank.Compared.To.Other.Countries-1005055.shtml.

3. http://www.oecd.org/dataoecd/27/11/35355743.pdf.

4. http://www.americanprogress.org/projects/progressivepriorities/files/Ch2-Health.pdf.

5. http://www.americanprogress.org/issues/2006/10/health_reports.html/pdf/health_lambrew.pdf.

6. Tom Daschle, "Trading Power for Progress: A Health Care 'Fed' to Reform Coverage," Center for American Progress, December 15, 2006.

CHAPTER 9
CREATING SUSTAINABLE SECURITY FOR AMERICA
AND THE WORLD

1. Gayle Smith, "Beyond Borders," *Democracy: A Journal of Ideas*, Winter 2007.

2. Paul Kennedy, *The Rise and Fall of the Great Powers*, Vintage, 1989.

3. Graham Allison, *Nuclear Terrorism: The Ultimate Preventable Catastrophe*, Times Books, 2004, pp. 44–45.

4. http://www.historyguide.org/europe/munich.html.

5. For more see http://www.americanprogress.org/issues/security/iraq.

6. David Herszenhorn, "Senate Democrats Focus on Costs of War," *New York Times*, February 27, 2008.

7. http://www.usatoday.com/news/washington/2006-08-01-guard-combat-read iness_x.htm.

8. http://www.usatoday.com/news/world/iraq/2004-03-26-body-armor_x.htm.

9. Shashi Tharoor, "Why America Still Needs the United Nations." *Foreign Affairs*, September/October 2003.

10. Bertrand Russell, *Freedom Versus Organization: 1814–1914*, Norton, 1934, pp. 450–451.

R esearching this book, I read many rich and detailed overviews of the original Populist, Progressive, New Deal, and Civil Rights eras. Many of my favorite accounts were written in the mid-1950s and 1960s and were geared toward a more general audience. For good narrative history of the early twentieth century reform movements, I suggest Eric Goldman's *Rendezvous with Destiny: A History of Modern American Reform*; George Mowry's *The Era of Theodore Roosevelt and the Birth of Modern America, 1900–1912*; and Robert Wiebe's *The Search for Order, 1877–1920*. The early editions of the *New Republic*, first published in 1914 and available in archives in most universities, also provide an interesting window into the contemporary thinking of Progressives during the era of Wilson and World War I. To read more critical assessments of the Progressive era, try Richard Hofstadter's *The Age of Reform*, or Michael McGerr's *A Fierce Discontent: The Rise and Fall of the Progressive Movement in America, 1870–1920*.

For the most detailed and informative accounts of the New Deal era, I suggest Arthur Schlesinger Jr.'s three-volume collection, *The Age of Roosevelt (Volumes I-III)*; David Kennedy's *Freedom From Fear: The American People in Depression and War, 1929–1945*; and William Leuchtenburg's *Franklin D. Roosevelt and the New Deal*. I also recommend Jonathan Alter's recent book, *The Defining Moment: FDR's Hundred Days and the Triumph of Hope.*

On the Civil Rights era, I enjoyed Taylor Branch's three-volume set on King, and David Garrow's *Bearing the Cross: Martin Luther King, Jr., and the Southern Christian Leadership Conference.* Kevin Mattson's *When America Was Great: The Fighting Faith of Postwar Liberalism,* provides a clear overview of the foreign policy fault lines and thinking that emerged after World War II and during the Cold War.

Beyond these more traditional sources, there are a few other books that I've enjoyed and used over the years. For a gripping account of how the troubles of American cities at the turn of the twentieth century led directly to progressive reform try David Von Drehle's *Triangle: The Fire That Changed America.* For a fascinating reconsideration of the influence of William Jennings Bryan, read Michael Kazin's *A Godly Hero: The Life of William Jennings Bryan.* For a great one-volume book of speeches and primary sources, see Caroline Kennedy, *A Patriot's Handbook: Songs, Poems, Stories and Speeches Celebrating the Land We Love.* For a fun fictional account of the era, read Caleb Carr's *The Alienist,* which takes place in New York in 1896 and features many historical figures mentioned in this book.

ACKNOWLEDGMENTS

There are many people who made the writing of this book possible, to whom I am grateful.

The idea for a book began in a conversation between my wonderful editor, Sean Desmond (with his colleague Julie Miesionczek), and Neera Tanden about collecting the best policy ideas the Center for American Progress had to offer to a new U.S. president. Neera, a CAP cofounder and brilliant policy analyst, found a more direct way to influence a possible president's agenda by signing on as Senator Hillary Clinton's policy director, but her early inputs and encouragement are reflected in this book.

After working on an early draft, it seemed to me that publishing a collection of policy proposals was like building a house without a foundation, because the ideas are rooted in history, values, and experience that need to be brought to the foreground, not left to assumption. So, I began to write a different book with the help of my colleague, John Halpin, a senior fellow at CAP. John is CAP's in-house progressive historian and he, along with the Glaser Progress Foundation, produced a series of ads about what it means to be a progressive that drew on the twentieth-century historical victories of the progressive movements. (See http://www.americanprogress .org/issues/2007/11/progressive_videos.html.)

We saw CAP's policy ideas emanating from a deep tradition of progressive leaders and thinkers stretching back to the late nineteenth century. I was familiar with the major figures who shaped this history, and John helped me appreciate some of the lesser-known theoreticians and activists of America's progressive past. John's research and analysis drove the historical chapters of this book. We both were aided enormously by the talent and friendship of David Dreyer and Charles Sweeney, who collaborated in the writing and editing of the text.

The policy prescriptions in the book are my own but reflect the enormous output of ideas, analyses, and critiques CAP has produced in the five years of its existence. That work simply would not have occurred if my friends and patrons, Herb and Marion Sandler, had not talked me into leaving full-time teaching at Georgetown University Law Center to head CAP. To them, Peter Lewis, Hansjorg Wyss, George Soros, and many other supporters, I owe a great debt of gratitude. Special thanks also to Richard Leone, president of The Century Foundation, and Professor Michael Kazin, my colleague at Georgetown University and author of a wonderful biography of William Jennings Bryan, A Godly Hero: The Life of William Jennings Bryan, for their input and comments.

Virtually every person who has worked at CAP helped shape this book, but I want to give special thanks to Sarah Wartell, who has been at CAP from day one and helped forge the economic chapter; Dr. Jeanne Lambrew on the health-care section; Todd Stern and Kit Batten on the climate and energy chapter; Gayle Smith, Rudy deLeon, Larry Korb, and Brian Katulis on the foreign policy chapter; and Melody Barnes, who guides CAP's overall policy direction. I want to thank Kathy Roche and Teresita Perez for making me seem more articulate than I am, and Juliana Gendelman for all her support to me and to this project.

The book, while not a memoir, became a reflection on my personal journey from a blue-collar Chicago neighborhood to working in the West Wing of the White House as President Clinton's chief of staff. It is an amazing journey in which I was blessed to have many mentors, friends, and guides. Any knowledge and wisdom I accumulated along the way are because of teachers like Harold Murray, who taught me the wonders of mathematics; Bob Shellenberger, from whom I learned the value of rigorous philosophical thinking; and Fathers Bill Byron, Jim Shea, and Jim Greenfield, who helped deepen my faith.

I have had wonderful political mentors, including three modern-day giants of the U.S. Senate, for whom I had the honor of working: Senator John Culver of Iowa, a former Marine whose son is now the state's successful governor, and who showed me what courage in the toughest political fights looks like; Senator Patrick Leahy of Vermont, whose love and fealty to the Constitution is as solid as the granite in his state; and Senator Tom Daschle, whose honor, decency, patience, and legislative skill not only earned him the respect of his colleagues on both sides of the aisle but also made him one of the longest-serving Democratic leaders in history.

No one was more inspiring and demanding of the best in me than Bill Clinton, the president I had the honor to serve. The public knows his political skills, intellect, tenacity, and ability to tell a story people can relate to, sometimes a very long story. I most admire two other things—his curiosity and his big heart. There simply is nothing the man is not interested in, whether it is the latest scientific development, health statistic from Africa, new jazz CD, crime novel, or college basketball score. And I know he is in public life for one reason—he loves to help people live good lives and believes politics and government are vehicles for doing that. Today, he continues that work through his foundation. The Clinton gravitational pull remains strong in the Podesta household. Our daughter Mae works in Africa on HIV/AIDS for the foundation.

Working for Bill Clinton enabled me to know another of the great leaders of progressive politics today—Hillary Clinton. She is and always will be an ideas politician, and her strong encouragement to me to start a progressive think tank led to the founding of CAP. But this spring, Hillary Clinton proved that behind her ideas burns a passion and commitment to the working Americans who are too often overlooked by conservative economics and conservative candidates. Hillary Clinton's historic campaign did not carry her to the White House, but her campaign has shined new light on the challenges faced by working Americans—people like my parents and grandparents—and proved that they, too, can be a critical part of a progressive coalition. And, as she returns to work as the U.S. Senate's most prominent progressive, she leaves behind a brilliant legacy for the women who will inevitably follow in her footsteps: eighteen million cracks in the ultimate glass ceiling.

There are countless others from whom I learned during the Clinton administration. I owe special thanks to Mack McLarty, who brought me there, and to the people in the second term who helped "run the joint," as my father would have said—my predecessor Erskine Bowles, Sylvia Mathews, with whom I served as co-deputy chief of staff to Erskine, and my deputies Maria Echaveste and Steve Richetti, and Karen Tramontano. And to the president's counselors, Rahm Emanuel and Doug Sosnik, and the policy advisers, Sandy Berger, Gene Sperling, Bruce Reed, and Jack Lew, who continue to be a source of policy ideas to me.

As I hope this book makes clear, the deepest lessons aren't that complicated—loyalty, honor, caring for one another, extending opportunities, and exalting the strengths and forgiving the weaknesses we see in each other. I learned them all at the kitchen table from my grandmother, who took care of me while my mother worked at night; from my father, who found pleasure in life's simplest things and I believe never made an enemy in his life; and from my mother, who passed away a year ago after a lifetime of nurturing and supporting not only her own family, but many virtual sons and daughters and friends she accumulated throughout her life. She could take a CTA bus ride, meet someone sitting next to her, and stay in touch for the rest of her life.

My brother Tony is a rock in my life—political guide, law-school classmate, business partner, confidant, best man, and godfather to my son. He was one of the first to fight back against right-wing intolerance when he and Norman Lear founded People for the American Way in 1980. With his wife, Heather, Tony continues to give time, money, and energy to the cause of Democratic politics and democratic change.

My wife and I have tried to instill in our children the values that we learned at home, especially the duty to see that everyone has a shot at success, the way we did. And we think we have succeeded. We long ago stopped being role models for Megan, Mae, and Gabe, and they, along with Megan's husband, Gordon, and our grandchildren, Maribel and Gabriel, are now role models for us. And for that, I thank them.

My wife Mary's life parallels my own in many ways, with her grandparents' journey beginning in Poland and ending in Central New Jersey. She, her brothers, and her sister grew up in the same kind of extended ethnic family that I did—that valued community, service, and responsibility to each other. Our similar backgrounds and values may explain why we have been great partners for thirty years. She is a world-class editor and contributed to this book. When I was a kid in the 1950s, I was a television fanatic, so perhaps it's fitting that I end here by saying to my wife, in the immortal words of Jackie Gleason in *The Honeymooners*, "Baby, you're the greatest."

INDEX

ABOUT THE CENTER FOR AMERICAN PROGRESS

The Center for American Progress (CAP) is a progressive think tank dedicated to improving the lives of Americans through ideas and action. CAP combines bold policy ideas with a modern communications platform to help shape the national debate, offer alternatives to conservative governing philosophy, and challenge the media to cover the issues that truly matter. Founded in 2003, CAP is headed by John D. Podesta, former chief of staff to President Bill Clinton and professor at the Georgetown University Center of Law.

CAP's policy experts cover a wide range of issue areas, and often work across disciplines to tackle complex, interrelated issues such as national security, energy, and climate change. This year, CAP is pushing to keep four leading issues at the center of the national debate:

- Restoring America's global leadership to make America more secure and build a better world.
- Seizing the energy opportunity to create a clean, innovation-led economy that supports a sustainable environment.
- Creating progressive growth that's robust and widely shared, and restoring economic opportunity for all.

- Delivering universal health care so that quality, affordable health services are available to all Americans.

How Can You Help?
Educate yourself on the issues and help inform the national debate by visiting www.americanprogress.org and our blog, www.thinkprogress.org. To stay informed on contemporary politics and policy, subscribe to the *Progress Report*, a daily review of the reality behind the news produced by the CAP Action Fund, CAP's sister advocacy organization.

Get involved in campus or state and local political issues shaping our collective future with the help of our online resources; do research, download policy papers, and make a difference.

Please consider donating to CAP's efforts as well. Without your generous support, we cannot do this important work. The Center for American Progress is a nonprofit, nonpartisan organization under section 501(c)(3) of the Internal Revenue code. Donations are tax-deductible.

Center for American Progress